More praise for
THE DOCTOR

"This is must reading for both patients and doctors. It's one of the rare health books that will be of equal benefit to both."

CONGRESSMAN RON WYDEN OF OREGON

"Dr. Rosenbaum gives a sensitive and compelling perspective of how real people, doctors and patients, deal with illness. A warm, inspiring book about being a doctor—and a patient."

CONGRESSMAN HENRY WAXMAN OF CALIFORNIA

"Must reading for physicians, nurses, hospital business office personnel, and anyone who ever sat on the patient's side of the bed."

DR. JOSEPH D. MATARAZZO
Chairman
Department of Medical Psychology
Oregon Health Sciences University

THE
DOCTOR

When the Doctor is the Patient

Dr. Edward E. Rosenbaum

Previously entitled: A TASTE OF MY OWN MEDICINE

IVY BOOKS • NEW YORK

TO MY GRANDCHILDREN
STEVE AND LAURA
LISA AND JENNIFER
SAM AND RACHEL

Ivy Books
Published by Ballantine Books
Copyright © 1988 by Edward E. Rosenbaum

Library of Congress Catalog Card Number: 87-32251

ISBN 0-8041-0873-0

This edition published by arrangement with Random House, Inc.

Printed in Canada

First Ballantine Books Edition: August 1991

PREFACE

I've been thinking lately about a conversation I had many, many years ago with my grandmother. I'd gone to her to tell her the wonderful news that I had been accepted at medical school. All she said was "Doctors are great—as long as you don't need them." I was very angry. I had expected her to be happy and proud of me, and I was surprised and shocked by her reaction.

It wasn't until years later, when I started practice, that I had a glimmer of what my grandmother meant. My first case was a house call on a man with a fever. Up until then, I had never been paid for my services, and when, at the end of the call, the patient asked, "How much?" I was embarrassed to answer him, so I quickly said, "Ten dollars." To my surprise, he seemed satisfied. He paid me, thanking me for my help, and I thought to myself, "What a crazy profession. I earn my living on other people's miseries." I'd told him he had the flu, though I wasn't sure I was right. And I knew that the truth was that he probably would have gotten well even if he had never seen me.

But money is a salve that quickly soothes the conscience. I continued to practice, and I prospered. I loved my profession, and we raised three of our sons to be doctors.

Over the years, when my children became ill, I would call a doctor because I knew a colleague who had treated his own son and failed to diagnose a perforated appendix. The father lived with that scar for the rest of his life.

When my wife became ill, I called a doctor because I knew of a pathologist who had treated his own wife and failed to diagnose cancer of the ovary. But whenever I got sick, I treated myself. Doctors were not for me. I realize now that, without verbalizing it, all my life I had avoided consulting them for my own medical problems because I was afraid of what they might tell me—and I knew their limitations. I had just been lucky. Eventually my day came, and I was trapped by what I must have known, almost from the start, was a grave illness.

When I became ill, like my patients, I wanted my doctors to be gods—and they couldn't be. But I also wanted them to understand my illness and my feelings and what I needed from my physicians. Those things they could have done—and some of them didn't.

I have heard it said that to be a doctor, you must first be a patient. In my own case, I practiced medicine for fifty years before I became a patient. It wasn't until then that I learned that the physician and the patient are not on the same track. The view is entirely different when you are standing at the side of the bed from when you are lying in it. If I could go back, I would do things in my own practice very differently than I did. Unfortunately, life doesn't give one that chance. All I can do is to tell you what happened to me and hope that we both can learn from it.

                                             —Edward E. Rosenbaum, M.D.

ACKNOWLEDGMENTS

To my wife, Davida, for her support and suggestions.

To my editor, Charlotte Mayerson, who taught me many things. I gave her crude raw material; she shaped and polished it. Without her this book would never have been.

To my typists, Kathy Johnson and Lucille Jette, for patiently typing and retyping.

To my patients who gave me years of trust and affection.

THE ONSET

On my seventieth birthday, I reported to the hospital to have a biopsy. I had practiced medicine at this hospital in Portland, Oregon, for more than forty years. I had been the chief of medicine and president of the staff; this year my eldest son, Richard, was president of the staff. On fifteen thousand previous visits I had entered through a private door like a king. I put on my light to notify the telephone operator that I was in the house, breezed past everyone with a cheery "good morning," and went up on an elevator marked PERSONNEL ONLY.

But today it was different. I was one of the common herd. I had to sit and wait my turn in the lobby for the admissions secretary to admit me. In spite of the fact that I had been at the hospital at least once a day for forty years, she asked my first name, my middle initial, my date of birth, nearest kin, whom to notify in an emergency, and, most important—my insurance carrier.

I had heard those questions thousands of times, but now they had a difference connotation. Religion meant "Do you want a clergyman? Will you want last rites?" Next of kin meant "Whom do we notify if the body has to be removed?" Insurance carrier meant "Who's going to pay for this?"

In the past, no patient whom I sent to the hospital had even been refused admission. Occasionally I would get a call from the business office notifying me that the patient had no insurance or was on welfare or that the insurance was exhausted. I would blandly reply, "I'll discuss it with the administrator tomorrow," and my patient was admitted. I had enough prestige to beat the system. With changing hospital economics and new administrations, I knew that my clout was ebbing away. In the future there would be nonemergency situations where I might be unable to have a patient admitted. And what would happen even now to the patient who had no physician to back him? Emergency means one thing to a hospital but something entirely different to the patient.

The waiting and typing took almost an hour and was extremely irksome. When I started practice, I knew a physician who specialized in caring for the wealthy. When he admitted patients to the hospital, he personally conducted them through the admissions process. He waved the secretaries aside, conducted the patient to the assigned room, and then went back himself to supply the necessary information to the admissions clerk. I used to laugh at such kid-glove treatment, but I now understood why those who could afford it were willing to pay that doctor's horrendous fees.

I had walked into the admitting room. There was no trouble with my legs; the problem was in my throat, but I had to go through the hospital ritual. I was not allowed to walk to my room; I had to be pushed in a wheelchair. Then I was subjected to the final indignity: they took away all my clothes and gave me a skimpy piece of cloth. I'm a pretty big guy, tall and, I've been told, barrel-chested. When I tied that piece of cloth around my neck, it wasn't long enough to cover the important parts. It was far too tight and hung open at the back. I felt as nude as a newborn baby and suddenly as helpless.

Lying in bed in a hospital room was a new experience too. I had been in similar rooms thousands of times, but in a different position. Then I was in command, neatly dressed, standing, looking down at a helpless patient in bed. Now I was that patient, literally stripped of my dignity. I was no longer in charge. I was being treated like a baby.

Later in the morning, as I began to settle down, the nurse came in with another paper for me to sign. It was a long legal document in fine print stating that I knew the risks of the surgery and anesthesia. I had already signed one such form at the admitting desk. That form relieved the hospital of responsibility; this form protected the surgeon and the anesthesiologist. Why it all couldn't have been done initially, I don't know.

I do understand the reason for the forms. Health care providers are worried about being sued, particularly since the courts have ruled that the patient must be fully informed of all risks and alternatives. But seldom are the forms explained; seldom are they even read.

My daughter-in-law Lois is a lawyer, and when she was in the hospital in labor, about to be sent to the delivery room, the nurse handed her a consent form. Lois protested. "All my training as an attorney forbids me to sign this without reading and understanding it." The startled nurse sent for the doctor to handle the difficult patient. The doctor spent a few minutes with Lois, gently explaining that the anesthesia could result in death or paralysis. Frightened, Lois looked helplessly at her husband, Richard, a physician, and he quietly said, "Sign it."

I signed my consent form too. What else was there to do? I had seen how useless it was to do anything else when one of my patients had been admitted for a hysterectomy. Although she had signed the consent form, because she was young, the surgeon demanded that her husband also sign it. The husband refused.

"Too-da-loo," said the surgeon. "Sign yourself out. Thursday is golf day. See you in the office tomorrow." With that, he left the hospital.

I didn't want to do anything to delay my own operation.

Though it was scheduled for noon, I had been ordered

to be at the hospital no later than seven in the morning. I was lucky; patients scheduled for eight had to report to the hospital at five A.M. For over a hundred years, the tradition has been to admit the patient the night before surgery, but in the last years, the procedure has changed. Many hospitals now admit the patient on the day of surgery, not because a scientific study has shown that this benefits the patient, but because it benefits the hospital. Hospitals are now paid by the case, not by the number of days. The fewer days the patient spends in the hospital, the more money the institution makes.

The admissions process had taken an hour, and then there were four anxious hours to kill. I tried to read but couldn't concentrate, so I talked to my wife about inane and unimportant things. At noon I was steeled to go when the nurse came with bad news: the surgical suite was ready but my surgeon was not; he was delayed by surgery at another hospital. The news was distressing. I was aware that surgeons scheduled their easy cases last, but now the surgeon was running behind, and he had added a commute between his major surgery and my operation. By the time he got to me he would be fatigued; he would rush the job in order to meet his afternoon appointments. I would get less than his best. It seemed to be a shabby way to treat a colleague.

It was approaching lunchtime, so I was also concerned about the anesthesiologist. The modern anesthesia machine is a complicated mechanism that can be driven only by an expert. I have known anesthetists to get hungry and step out into the hall for a sandwich and a glass of orange juice while the machine is turned over to an assistant and put on automatic pilot. But Richard had picked my anesthetist. I knew someone picked by my son would not do that to me.

Richard had called the evening before. He'd asked about the biopsy, and I'd assured him, "Don't worry. It's minor surgery."

"I know," he replied. "And your doctor, Al Cade, is

good. The risk isn't the surgery, the risk is the general anesthesia."

"You're right," I agreed. "I wasn't thinking and left the choice of the anesthesiologist to Al." Then I proceeded to lecture Richard: "When I was a senior medical student, tonsillectomies under local anesthesia were common. I witnessed one operation where the surgeon injected one tonsil and the sixteen-year-old slumped over dead. The new student nurse had filled the syringe with cocaine instead of novocaine, which was the usual local anesthesia used at that time.

"In World War II, pentothal was a new intravenous anesthetic. We enthusiastically used enlisted men to inject the drug while the doctors operated. Later we realized that some of the wounded were dying from anesthesia and not from surgery.

"I've known of patients who were given a preoperative injection of morphine and never reached the operating table. Was it error of dosage or unusual sensitivity to a drug? We'll never know."

"So why don't you call Uncle Bill?" Rick asked, interrupting my tirade. "He's in the operating room every day, he knows all the anesthetists."

Bill is my brother and a very active surgeon. "I wish I could reach him," I told Richard. "He's away fishing, and you know what happens when he goes fishing . . . he puts on his old black felt hat, puts a feather in it, goes out with one of his Indian friends, and when he gets up on Mt. Hood and smells the fish, he forgets everything else. He's up there now, and I doubt if he'll be home before midnight. You're important, you have clout, you're president of the staff. Get the best anesthetist you can."

Later Richard called back. He had selected an anesthesiologist to handle my case personally, and now, waiting in the hospital room, despite my worries about the anesthetist's lunch, I said to my wife, "It pays to have a son for a doctor. I feel secure. I have a good surgeon and the top anesthetist."

At last it was time for the surgery. The nurse came into my room and treated me like a child. I know she meant well, but it was embarrassing. She wasn't more than twenty-five years old. I had always been her boss, and now she was telling me what to do. Without asking my permission, she removed the sheet covering me, and there I lay on the bed, almost completely naked. All I had on was this hospital gown which reached only to my belly button. She wanted to help me onto the cart, but I wouldn't let her; I wasn't helpless yet. When I was settled on the cart, she again covered me with the thin sheet that I was sure everyone could see through, and I was wheeled down the hall to the elevator. There were other passengers in the elevator and they all looked down on me, and again I felt naked. By the time I got down to the operating room I was almost glad to see the anesthetist. He greeted me, started an intravenous at once, and then I was asleep.

When I awoke, I was in the recovery room and everyone was all smiles. One of the young, pretty nurses was holding my hand. It was such a pleasant sensation that it confirmed my certainty that the anesthesia had not damaged my body or brain.

Shortly after I was returned to my room, the surgeon came to see me. He was cheerful and reassuring. He had found a small polyp, and without benefit of a pathological examination, he assured me that it was benign.

I was not reassured, though a layperson might have been. I knew better. I had learned when I was an intern that a surgeon cannot determine the presence or absence of cancer by looking at the gross specimen; a microscopic examination is essential.

The patient was Al Kendall, a burly Irish fireman, forty-five years old and in the prime of his life. It was the first week of my internship in St. Louis. I was twenty-three years old, idealistic, and convinced that doctors were infallible. I was scrubbing with a world-famous surgeon who opened the patient's abdomen, took one look inside, raised his hands and said, "Inoperable. Cancer." He quickly stopped the operation, closed the abdomen and sent the patient back to his room to die.

Since I was the youngest doctor on the team, my elders decided it would be a good experience for me to tell the bad news to the family. Medical school had not prepared me for this; I didn't know where to start. I found the wife, a petite Irish colleen with big brown eyes and brown hair, anxiously waiting in the hall. As gently as I could, I told her that her husband had inoperable cancer. First she stared at me in shock, and then, as she recovered, silent tears rolled down her cheeks. She reached over to hold my hands and asked, "How long does he have to live?"

"At the most, six months," I told her, and then I left, wondering why I had ever wanted to be a doctor.

A year later, I met Mrs. Kendall on the street.

"How are things going?" I asked her, really meaning, when did your husband die?

She understood and answered, "Al is well, back working as a fireman."

"What happened?"

"We just waited, but when six months passed and he was still alive, we went to another doctor who reoperated. You were wrong. Al never had cancer. He had an inflammation of the pancreas."

That early experience taught me never to offer a prognosis, and never to make or believe a diagnosis of cancer without benefit of a microscopic examination of tissue. I have learned that it is not given to man to prognosticate the duration of a life. I have known doctors to advise the patient and the family that the outlook is hopeless, and yet the patient survives. Are these recoveries miracles? I don't think so, but on the other hand, I cannot explain them.

My own illness had started six months before my surgery. My voice seemed to be changing. So what? I had a little cold, and I was getting older. Everyone gets a cold. But colds clear up in a few days; mine did not. My hoarseness persisted. I couldn't ignore the hoarseness, but I was too busy to see a doctor. My wife nagged until, reluctantly, I kept the appointment that she had made with our friend, Dr. Al Cade, a nose and throat specialist.

It took the doctor five minutes to look into my throat with a mirror and pat me on the back. "I don't see much, Ed. Probably a little cold. Take an antibiotic if you aren't allergic. Try some penicillin. Here are some samples. I'll also give you samples of allergy pills. Try them, they're effective. And try steam inhalations."

I liked him; he told me what I wanted to hear. I just went home, threw the samples in the garbage can, didn't buy a steamer, didn't take the penicillin. My hoarseness persisted.

"No wonder you're no better," my wife said. "You haven't done a thing the doctor told you."

"I don't believe in doctors," I explained. "Sometimes they give you medicine when they don't know what else to do, and I don't believe in using penicillin lightheartedly—especially not for a cold, which it doesn't help. The stuff can be poison if you take it when you don't need it."

In February my hoarseness returned, but I knew I wasn't sick. I had no fever, no pain, and no lack of appetite, and my doctor had said that I was okay. No, I was sure I was healthy, the sick one was my wife. She had a fever, a cough, and fatigue.

I had a right to worry about her. It had been a long time since she had had a breast removed for cancer, and I was concerned. Maybe the cancer had spread to the lung. I insisted that she see a lung specialist. He X-rayed her chest, and, as I feared, there were spots in the lung. He recommended a bronchoscopic examination of the lungs.

"We must be sure that she does not have cancer," he explained, and I agreed.

Then I did what doctors frequently do when they themselves get sick. To avoid the tension and delays involved in a regular office visit, they corner a colleague in the hall or over a cup of coffee and describe their symptoms. In the profession, it's called a curbstone consultation. It's free, quick, painless—and often worthless. While I was in the doctor's office, and without benefit of a formal appointment, I gathered up my courage to say, "As long as you're looking at her, take a look at me. I seem to have a persistent hoarseness."

Although he was busy and I did not have an appointment, this second physician courteously ordered a chest X ray, viewed the film, and pronounced it normal. Then he poked an instrument into my throat, examined the larynx quickly, and removed the instrument. He sprayed my throat with a local anesthetic, looked again carefully, and told me, "There's nothing to worry about." I was relieved; two doctors had assured me that there was no cause for alarm, and I had gotten the worry off my mind without the need of going through a routine appointment.

My wife's examination was more thorough; under sedation her lungs were bronchoscoped, a procedure that I would not have wanted to go through. The doctor reassured us, "Neither of you has cause for concern."

My wife's fever and cough disappeared, but my hoarseness lingered. I wasn't sick; I knew that I did not have anything serious. Two specialists had told me so. I knew that they were good because I referred patients to them.

Although the hoarseness persisted, I continued to practice. By March, patients often commented, "You sound terrible," and with concern some asked, "Are you sick?"

I knew that a cold could not be causing my problem. It had gone on too long. But even though I knew better, I told my friends and my family that there was no cause for concern and avoided pursuing the problem any further. Why look for trouble?

Finally, in desperation, Dee, without asking my permission, made an appointment with Dr. Cade. Because I

was anxious, in spite of my pretended nonchalance, I arrived too early. The doctor treated me like a colleague.
Though the reception room was full, I was taken out of
turn. He assured me with a smile, a handshake, and the
third examination of my vocal cords. "Nothing wrong,"
he said. "Maybe a little swelling, maybe a little inflammation, but nothing to worry about. Are you taking penicillin and steaming?"

"No," I confessed.

"No wonder you're no better," he gently chided me.
Then he reached into his drawer to hand me another batch
of samples.

"Al," I laughed, "keep those for your patients. You
can fool them, but not me. If this is a simple cold, nothing
you have in that drawer will cure me. All I need to be
sure of is that I don't have a cancer."

"It might not cure you, but it might make you feel
better," Al persisted.

"You remind me of Davy Goodman," I told him.
"Davy and I were in the same outfit in the army. He was
from New Jersey and a little older than the rest of us, who
were fresh out of our residencies. He delighted in telling
us how practice was in the real world outside the hospital.
In those days a major infant problem was diarrhea, and
there was no specific medical treatment. Davy said his
method was: 'When the mother consults you, tell her to
give the baby chicken soup. Advise her that the soup must
be made from a chicken that is exactly eight days old, not
seven days, not nine days, but exactly eight days old. She
will spend a day searching in the markets, and you will
avoid frantic calls. By the time she calls you back, the
baby will be well.'

"Al, don't treat me like a patient. Treat me like a doctor." I insisted.

Even though the waiting room was full, Al spent the
next fifteen minutes telling me of a partnership he had
formed to market a new medical device.

I left elated; I liked Al. I knew that I did not have

cancer, and my colleague had treated me like a doctor deserved to be treated.

I should have had a sense of foreboding when Dr. Cade took me out of turn, for I have treated many a doctor and their families, and I know that to treat them differently than other patients is to invite an error.

A week later, Al stopped by my office to see how I was doing. Yes, I thought, I was getting special attention, but after all, I had referred many a patient to Dr. Cade. Again, we were both allowing irrelevant "professional" considerations to set the course of my diagnosis and treatment.

"I'm no better," I told him.

"I've brought you the latest treatment," he said. "Your problem may be allergic. Try this cortisone inhaler."

"No way," I said. "It's not for me. I've been prescribing cortisone for years. It's dynamite, full of side effects. I use it less and less every year, and only when there is no other choice."

"This is a new way to take it, so that you don't get the side effects. You inhale it."

Against my better judgment, I used the cortisone inhaler for ten days. I desperately wanted to get better, so I convinced myself that it was helping. I wanted whatever was wrong with me to be an allergic problem. But in truth, the hoarseness did not go away.

In April my jaw hurt, and I went to a new young dentist. He tapped my teeth, X-rayed them, and said, "Your teeth are good; your bite's off."

I said to my wife, "All these years I have been going to dentists and none of them have found a problem with my bite. This guy is really smart. He's modern, up to date."

With my consent, the dentist ground one molar and said, "Now you'll be all right."

I went home and wasn't all right; the pain persisted. I waited a week and went back to the dentist, who again said, "Your teeth are okay; your bite's off."

He ground more off the molar, rechecked my bite and assured me, "Now you'll be all right."

I went home and slept for two nights pain-free, but the pain returned on the third night. Back I went for more grinding, and two days later I awoke on a Saturday morning with a toothache and spit out half a tooth!

"My," the dentist said when he saw me, "I've been grinding on the wrong tooth!" Finally he sent me to a specialist for a root canal treatment; the tooth was gone.

Soon the dentist's bill arrived, three hundred dollars for three visits. I wasn't going to pay it, but I got to wondering how many times I had seen patients without making a diagnosis or prescribed a drug to which my patients reacted inappropriately. Yet I still sent a bill. In fact, I once got a letter from a woman who wrote, "Doctor, when I was in the hospital, my doctor called you in consultation. You thought I was in a coma, but I really wasn't. You were fooled because my eyes were closed. I heard what you said. You stood at the foot of my bed and said to my doctor, 'I don't know, I just don't know.' Doctor, this will be the first medical bill in my life that I will not pay. I am willing to pay for what you know, but not for what you don't know."

The memory made me pay the dentist's bill.

After the endodontist performed the root canal on my tooth, he advised me to take some penicillin prophylactically to prevent a tooth abscess. Now I had a double reason for taking the penicillin: persistence of my hoarseness and the advice of the dentist. Reluctantly, I took it.

I was well acquainted with penicillin. Prior to World War II, pneumonia was the leading cause of death, and there was no effective treatment. In 1944 I was ordered by the army to a hospital in Oxford, England, to witness a new secret weapon. A London bobby was dying of pneumonia. He was given one injection of penicillin, and the next day he was on his way to recovery. Later I was in the invasion of Normandy and was decorated with a Bronze Star for my work in administering penicillin to wounded soldiers.

As time went on, penicillin's flaws were revealed. Some

bacteria became resistant to the antibiotic, and penicillin was no longer effective. Hospitals where penicillin was overused became cesspools of infection because the organisms sensitive to penicillin were destroyed, while those that were resistant became dominant. Staphylococcal skin infections were prevalent in such institutions. I know of one infant death labeled "crib death" that I believe was due to an allergic reaction to penicillin. The penicillin was given to treat a simple cold by an overenthusiastic pediatrician.

Often patients with common colds insist on "shots of penicillin." As I have gained experience, I have resisted these demands, as I know that penicillin is of no value in treating the simple cold. I personally have treated severe allergic reactions, skin reactions, and diarrhea secondary to unnecessary use of penicillin. Despite all this, it is often difficult to convince the patient that the penicillin is unnecessary.

Hospitals have monitoring committees to police the practice and use of antibiotics, but outside of the hospital physicians are on their own. I was determined not to take penicillin if I could possibly avoid it. As a doctor, I made the judgment that the penicillin was not indicated for my hoarseness, but I had no expertise in dentistry. The dentist insisted that I had an abscess and was in danger of developing a severe infection that could be prevented by the penicillin. I reluctantly complied and took it with no results. It took another six weeks of persistent hoarseness before I got to this hospital bed.

I left the hospital in the afternoon after the exploratory surgery and awoke at home the following morning, anxiously waiting to learn the pathologist's opinion. After a while, I was so restless I went outside and paced the garden to relieve the tension. Finally, at noon, Dee came outside to tell me that Dr. Cade had called. The pathologist had interpreted the tissue slides as benign. I have known pathologists to disagree, and I have known pathological slides to be labeled benign and later prove to be malignant, or vice versa, but in this case I didn't allow myself such doubt. I liked the report, and I was at ease.

After the surgery my voice was worse, and when the hoarseness continued for a few weeks, I called my doctor. "Don't worry," he said, "vocal cords heal slowly. Soon you will talk normally." I assured my friends, my family, and my patients that I was well, but the speech problem persisted.

Free advice was plentiful.

"Stop talking."

"Drink cactus juice."

"Take a vacation."

Everyone had a different suggestion. I continued to croak, but I liked the free advice, because it assured me that my friends were concerned. As a practicing doctor, I resented the advice patients got from relatives, friends, and strangers. In my generation and even to a large degree today, a doctor's word is law, not to be questioned. I have often said to patients, "I have spent a lifetime treating your disease. If I'm not sure what to do, how can your neighbor know? I have a license, they don't." Then I would hand them pamphlets published by the American Medical Association. The literature would explain why they should listen to me and not to other kinds of healers.

Olive Jensen, one of my arthritis patients, was a doctor's mother. As a courtesy to her son, I did not charge her a fee. To repay me, at Christmastime she presented me with a little gift—six copies of one book in which the author said that because he was not a doctor but a laboratory technician, he understood bodily fluids better. He advised copious amounts of cod liver oil to lubricate the joints. I suppose Mrs. Jensen gave me so many copies so I would distribute them to my patients. I was really annoyed at the time, but now, for the first time, I understood Mrs. Jensen's gift. She had been impaired for months, and I had not helped her. No wonder she looked elsewhere.

In my own case, I had had three examinations and surgery, and my hoarseness was getting worse. So I read everything I could in the lay press. It took all my willpower not to send the articles to Dr. Cade, but knowing my own kind, I didn't want to insult him.

Two months after surgery I was no better, but I didn't seek a second opinion. I was violating a basic rule: "Get a second opinion if you are not responding in a reasonable period of time." It was now long past a reasonable period of time.

Instead I tried cough drops, six boxes of them. I would have scolded a patient who did that, but my case was different. I had already seen two doctors—and the cough drop advice came from a physician, after all. One night at a dinner party Dr. Rian took pity on me because I couldn't talk to her. She gave me some of her cough drops. They were very special, she assured me, she had used them since childhood. The drops weren't available in pharmacies, only in health food stores. I had Dee get them for me, so that I wouldn't be seen buying them. It was only after the sixth package that I gave up and called Dr. Cade.

After listening to me he said, "There is nothing wrong with your vocal cords. It's psychological. I'll send you to a speech clinic at the medical school."

I really knew better. Too often doctors use that diagnosis to hide their failings, but again I liked the opinion. It meant that I had a manageable disorder.

My father had taught me that emotions do affect illnesses. Dad suffered from crippling headaches. Every few weeks he would be stricken, and on bad days he would have to leave his work servicing cars at our gas station on Twenty-second and Burt Street in Omaha. My mother would relieve him at the pumps, and he would retreat to a back room, slump into a chair among barrels of oil and grease, pull the shades down, cover his head with a damp towel, and suffer for the day.

When her two boys were in school and her husband was sick, my mother would work the gas station by herself. In those days, the gas pumps were not electrified. She pumped them by hand, and she didn't object to getting her hands greasy. If a motorist drove into our station and it was necessary to clean the carburetor or change the spark plugs, she did it. The men would just stand by shaking their heads, watching her in disbelief. I was embarrassed. Who else's mother would get their hands greasy doing a man's job? Certainly no other Jewish mother. But she insisted that she could do any work that a man could do, and she told me, "There is no disgrace in doing menial, dirty work as long as it's honest."

In 1934, when I was nineteen, Dad was having one of those bad headache days. Mother and I were at the gas pumps when *the* important letter came: I had been accepted to medical school! In those days it was hard for a Jew to get into medical school. All the schools openly admitted that they had strict Jewish quotas. To be Jewish and get into medical school meant excelling academically, but even that was not enough. A Jew could be eliminated by a whim of the admissions committee: "He's not a gentleman" or "He's not our kind."

When I read the news, I rushed to the back room to tell my father. His headache disappeared at once. He threw the wet rag aside, opened the windows, and went back outside to join us at work.

"Pop," I told him, "I need a twenty-five-dollar deposit to reserve my place."

"Don't worry," he assured me, "I'll find the money someplace."

"Tuition is two hundred dollars a year," I reminded him.

"We'll make it."

"How?"

"I'll work harder," Dad said.

"Pop, you already work seven days a week, from seven in the morning till ten at night. All you do is work, eat, and sleep. How are you going to work harder?"

"I'll open the station at six A.M. We're missing some of the early morning business."

"What about your headaches?"

"When my oldest son is a doctor, I won't have any more headaches."

I was lucky I was born in Omaha. If I had been born in New York and had to compete with a large Jewish population, it would have been tougher to get into medical school. My grandparents settled in Omaha at the turn of the century. They originally came from a small village in the Ukraine. They passed through Ellis Island and settled in New York, but coming from a small town, they were unable to adjust to the new culture and the big city. They worked in sweatshops only long enough to accumulate enough money for a railroad ticket, then pushed ahead to Omaha to join relatives and *landsmen* from their village. In Omaha there were no tall buildings, no apartment houses or tenements. As poor as they were, each family had a house and a yard to itself. Anti-Semitism existed, but it was not overt. Jews voluntarily segregated themselves into their own neighborhoods so that they could be near their butchers, ritual bathhouses, and synagogues.

When I was growing up in Omaha, it was a city of two hundred thousand, with ten thousand Jews. The city limit was Sixtieth Street, and I would ride with my grandfather in his wagon to neighboring farms to buy fresh fruit and vegetables. There were three Orthodox synagogues, a Reform temple, and a Conservative congregation. The community was closely knit and saw to it that none of its members fell upon public charity.

Most of the first generation of Jewish families were employed as peddlers, junk dealers, ragpickers, and small shopkeepers. Some of their children got jobs as salesmen, or in department stores or with the railroad, but government, banking, and big business were closed to them. As to the professions, law was open to them, medicine and dentistry were restricted by quotas, and to get a job as an engineer was impossible. No one at that time could possibly have foreseen that someday I would be the physician to members of the university admissions committee, or that my four sons would all earn degrees at Harvard or Yale.

Though I accepted the diagnosis that my illness was psychological, I knew that diagnosis could at times hide horrible errors. When my own nephew Billy was fifteen years old, his personality had changed. He had always been a kind boy with an interest in nature and science. Suddenly he lost interest in school, argued incessantly with his sisters, and defied his parents. I sent him to a neurologist, who assured the family that it was all mental; he was a typical teenager going through adolescent problems. A psychiatrist agreed. For three months Billy was treated by psychotherapy. Then, when he began to develop physical changes, the diagnosis became obvious. Within six months, he was dead of a brain tumor.

My own diagnosis didn't make sense. I was comfortable with my practice, my family and my world, but I accepted Dr. Cade's opinion that my illness was psychological, and I kept an appointment at the speech clinic, where I had never been before, even though I had started teaching internal medicine and cardiology at the medical school in 1948. At that time my later interest, rheumatology, was not considered a legitimate medical specialty. There was little that could be done for the patient with rheumatic disease, so doctors felt that it was best left to the quacks. But in 1950, with the discovery that cortisone could influence rheumatic diseases, rheumatology became a recognized specialty. Having spent time at the Mayo Clinic with Dr. Phil Hench, who shared the Nobel Prize for discovering cortisone, I was among the few physicians in the United States formally trained in the treatment of rheumatic diseases. I was the founder of the rheumatology clinic at University of Oregon Health Sciences University, and as the years progressed and my reputation spread in the Northwest, I began to treat more arthritis and fewer and fewer cases of general medicine.

I'd never had any reason even to think about the speech clinic. As soon as I crossed the campus and entered the waiting room, I felt out of place. The room was full of children, mothers, and toys. While I was debating whether to walk out, the speech therapist took me firmly in tow, and I found myself following her down the hall. She sat me down in a small private room, and her first question was "Do you recognize me?"

I had to admit that I didn't.

"I had arthritis and was a patient of yours twenty years ago."

I didn't answer. This situation always made me uneasy, because I know that arthritis is seldom cured. I suspected that I had failed the woman—and now it was my turn to be *her* patient.

The therapist began by making a tape recording of my voice. Then she instructed me to lead a clean life: no smoking, limited alcohol, exercise, wholesome diet, ten glasses of water a day, relax, use a cold-water vaporizer in my bedroom.

Although I don't smoke or drink, I do weigh too much and don't exercise, so I agreed to cooperate. "You're right," I told her. "I'll walk every day, I'll get the vaporizer, and I'll relax."

I decided to be a model patient and to start by exercising. I was never a great one for physical exertion. I used to begin the day by walking around my garden before I left for the office, and I would complete my daily exercise program by walking around the garden a second time when I came home in the evening. All in all, I probably walked about three thousand steps, admiring my roses, azaleas, rhododendrons, camellias, bamboo, and magnolias. In Portland's mild climate, the camellias start blooming in February. By April the flowers on the rhododendrons are as big as coconuts, and by mid-May the azaleas and magnolias and flowering cherries have joined in the parade.

Then the city is a blaze of color. Even in the poorest neighborhoods, the yards are all abloom. In July the back part of my garden is lush with fruits and vegetables. Cherries, berries, and nuts thrive here. The Bing cherry originated in the northwest, and we produce much of the nation's supply of Royal Annes, which are used to make maraschino cherries. In December we begin to harvest the Christmas trees, and much of the country's holly is grown within a few miles of my home.

Now that I had reformed, I decided to extend my usual walk. Portland has 179 parks. Across the street from my house is Hoyt Arboretum, which has twenty-three miles of hiking trails and trees from all over the world. As you enter the coolness of the forest, you feel as if you are in a wilderness; there are few hikers, no automobiles, and no city. On my new program, I walked the shaded paths along sparkling streams, I heard bird sounds that I had never heard before, and I realized that even though the park was across the street from where we've lived for thirty years, I had rarely been on these trails; I had been too busy. I was reminded of a story I read of a gardener who felt sorry for his master. The owner had to get up every morning at seven o'clock to go to the city to earn enough so that the gardener could enjoy the grounds. I realized that I, too, had been making that mistake. I had been so engrossed and dedicated to my work that I had been missing the world around me.

Still, though I did everything the therapist told me to do, I wasn't any better. At the next visit I asked her why.

"Because you are not relaxed," she answered.

"I've never been more relaxed in my life."

"I'll show you," she answered. "Here, feel how tight this muscle is in your neck." And she placed my hand on a neck muscle.

"You're right," I said. I really didn't notice any difference in the muscles, but I didn't want to hurt her feelings. That was dumb, but it is a common reaction of patients: don't upset the doctor or he or she won't like you and

won't take good care of you. I was startled by that insight.
Had I know that before? Would it have changed my relationship with my patients? I wasn't sure.

When I returned for the third appointment, the medical
director of the speech clinic, Dr. DuVall, was there. I
wondered why. I hadn't asked for him.

"I'm going to make movies of your vocal cords," he
explained to me, "and then we'll see what you're doing
wrong and we'll be able to train you to use your voice
properly."

He attached a thin, flexible tube with a light on one end
to a camera. I opened my mouth wide, and he inserted a
light into my throat and started the camera. I could tell
from the horrified look on the therapist's face and the doctor's frown that something was wrong. He removed the
instrument and then showed me the movies of my vocal
cords. The pictures magnified the lesion. I could see the
red, inflamed cords and a huge ulcer. I felt sick to my
stomach, like the way I had felt the first day of medical
school when I stuck a knife into a cadaver. Years of training had inured me to the sight of blood and gore, but this
was different; this was me. I was back to day one.

Then the doctor gently said, "You have a tumor," and
added, "it may respond to X ray." Though he hadn't said
the word, I knew what he meant; I had cancer. I myself
had seen that ugly ulcer. There wasn't any treatment I
knew of that could affect that.

If DuVall had followed the accepted medical custom, he
wouldn't have said a word to me. He would have advised me
to make an appointment with my referring physician for reexamination. Then, privately, he would have informed my
doctor of the correct diagnosis so I, the patient, would not
be aware of the error my own doctor had made.

But as distressing as the news was, I appreciated not
going through the usual ritual. I knew that this probably
would cost DuVall a source of patient referrals, for Dr.
Cade would never again send a patient to him. But DuVall
was following a better rule, one that a wise professor once

taught me: "What's ethical is what's best for the patient, not what's good for the doctor."

"You'll need a more thorough examination," DuVall continued. "I'll meet you at my private office in half an hour. Have my secretary register you and prepare a chart."

As I walked across the campus, I understood I was getting special care, not what the ordinary patient would receive. I didn't have to go through the registration procedures, and the doctor was interrupting his schedule for my examination. Still, I resented him and was reluctant to believe him.

I went over the facts in my mind. It's true that I was hoarse, but I wasn't sick. Two excellent senior physicians had previously assured me that I had only a minor throat problem. I was at the medical school for voice therapy to improve my speech, not to see a doctor.

Now this young guy, thirty years my junior, had the temerity to raise the possibility of cancer. What right did he have to do that? I'm the doctor. I tell people they have cancer, but no one says that to me. Doctors are immune; they don't get sick.

He's young, inexperienced, overzealous and wants to impress me. I should never have come to the medical school. No one can tell whether or not there's a cancer by merely looking. This kid hasn't even done a biopsy yet!

As I regained my senses, I thought about him again. He was young, tall, angular, blue-eyed, with a full head of hair and a closely cropped beard, no gray. He looked impressive, like a TV soap opera doctor, but I didn't like him. He was telling me something that I never expected and didn't want to hear.

After all, I am an internist of fifty years' experience and protected by nine doctors in the immediate Rosenbaum family. My eldest son, Richard, is a neurologist. My second son, Jimmy, is a rheumatologist; his wife, Sandra, a cardiologist. My third son, Howard, and his wife, Marcia, are both psychiatrists. (My fourth son, Kenny, a maverick, is an attorney.)

I practice with my brother, Bill, who is a surgeon. His eldest son, Robert, is a neurologist. His second son, Tom, is a neurosurgeon.

I don't smoke, I rarely drink, my mother-in-law is one of the best cooks in the world, so I get plenty of good food, and my wife, Dee, was trained as a dictician, so we know what to eat.

Medical superstition has it that doctors die of the disease they specialize in. I am a rheumatologist. People seldom die of a rheumatic disease.

No way could I have cancer. I must have misunderstood. Doctors and nurses speak a queer language. They use words that mean one thing to them, something else to patients.

Years ago, when I worked in a busy hospital emergency room, the nurses placed the patients in tiny cubicles. To save the doctor's time, nurses recorded on the chart the subject's vital signs: temperature, pulse, blood pressure, and respirations. On one particularly busy night, I walked into a cubicle to find an elderly man on the examining table. The nurse rushed in after me and breathlessly insisted, "Doctor, wait! Don't see him. I haven't gotten to his vitals yet." The man leaped off the table, clutching his crotch, and said, "Lady, no way you're going to touch me!"

I wondered if that could have happened to me. Did the doctor say that I had a growth or did he say I had cancer? Maybe I didn't hear him right. This can't be happening. Doctors are the handmaidens of God. They earn their immunity from the ordinary problems of life.

I have gone wherever I was needed. I have cared for all comers, rich or poor, all races, all religions, and during the war, even the wounded enemy. I have defended my profession. I have reared my sons to be doctors. They have married doctors. Surely God has not turned on me.

When we met in his office, DuVall examined me in a way I had never been examined before. First I lay down on a narrow table. He sprayed a bitter anesthetic in my throat that made me cough and spit. After waiting ten minutes for the anesthetic to take effect, he took out of an antiseptic solution a strange instrument, a long, narrow tube about the diameter of a soda straw. On one end was a tiny light, and on the opposite end the tube was expanded into what appeared to be an eyepiece. I'd never seen one before and certainly had never been trained to use one.

"What are you using on me?" I asked.

"A fiberoptic nasopharyngoscope," he answered. Without further conversation, he passed the tube through my nose and down into my throat. As gentle as he was, I gagged. He spent five minutes looking through the eyepiece and moving the instrument up and down and side to side. He had me pronounce the vowels "eeeeeeeeeee, aaaaaaaaaaaaah." I could hardly croak the syllables. He finally withdrew the tube.

We sat down in his consultation room as he outlined the procedure. "You will have a general anesthetic, and I will repeat the biopsy."

"You think it's malignant?" I said.

"I wouldn't be subjecting you to the risk of a second operation if I didn't think so." He had a serious look on his face. "You will need an electrocardiogram, a chest X ray, a complete blood count, a blood chemistry screen, and urine tests before the operation." He handed me the necessary appointment slips.

"Why did the first two doctors miss the diagnosis?"

"Did they use a fiberoptic pharyngoscope?"

"No," I said, "they did it with mirrors, the way I was taught and the only way I knew existed."

"For the last four years," DuVall explained, "we have been using this instrument. It's much better because it gives us a direct look. Your lesion is underneath the cord. There isn't any way that it can be visualized by the mirrors. Many of the older men still haven't learned to use this instrument." Then he said, very definitely, "I'll treat you with Xray."

That frightened me. To me, X ray meant palliation. It meant my case was hopeless. A patient in my practice had had his vocal cords removed. He was alive; he had no voice, but he was alive. X ray? I thought to myself, X ray causes cancer. All the early X-ray men died of cancer from exposure to the rays. Now this man was proposing Xray therapy to me. I had stopped using X-ray therapy a long time ago with my own patients.

"Look," I told him, "don't awaken me from the anesthesia. Forget about the Xray. If the frozen section biopsy is positive, go ahead with the surgery. What's the use of waking me up and putting me to sleep again? I'm a doctor; you don't need signed consent from me."

"No," he said. "I want you awake so we can discuss alternative treatment. X ray may be better than surgery."

We walked out into the reception room. He grasped my hands. "Wait here awhile," he said. "My secretary will arrange the time for your surgery. I am sorry we had to meet under these circumstances."

I was still dazed by the news. I called Dee, my wife, and made no attempt to soften the blow. I told her everything and she said, "I can't talk to you right now, I'm too busy."

In forty-three years of marriage, that was the only time that she had ever said that. Usually she accused me of not communicating enough. I wondered why I had told her the news so directly. In the past, when something happened, I have either avoided telling her or softened the bad news. Then I realized that I had been abrupt because for the first time in my life I felt that I was not in control. My destiny was no longer in my hands.

Five minutes later she called me back. "I can only talk to you for a minute," she said. "I'm at my bridge club now and I have a very good hand." Then I repeated the morning's events. She offered no comment.

I understood Dee's reaction. The word cancer is so terrifying that we seek refuge. When I was a Fellow at the Mayo Clinic, thousands of cases of cancer of the stomach were treated. Yet when one of the senior physicians developed stomach cancer, he insisted that he not be treated on the same floor as the other cancer patients and demanded that only one doctor see him; he did not want to be told the diagnosis.

We dread the word cancer. When I practiced cardiology, one of my patients had a severe, pressing chest pain and then broke into a cold sweat. By the time the ambulance arrived at the hospital, he was in shock.

I stayed with him through the night, but by dawn I knew that my efforts were in vain. I went out to see the anxious family waiting in the hallway. "He won't make it," I said. "He had a severe heart attack."

"How much longer?" asked the son.

"I don't know," I shook my head again. "He's in shock; it won't be long."

It took time for the message to sink in. Finally his wife responded, "Thank God he doesn't have a cancer."

By now the doctor's secretary was ready for me. "The surgical schedule is full for Monday," she said. "We have to see if we can schedule you on Tuesday. The secretary who does the Tuesday scheduling is not available now. We'll have to wait until she comes back."

So I sat and I waited for forty-five minutes. I thought, If it takes an hour to schedule an operation here, and if one girl schedules Monday and another secretary schedules Tuesday, how efficient is this hospital? Besides, this is Friday. Tuesday is three days off. Every minute of delay gives the cancer cells a chance to spread to other parts of the body. If that occurs, no matter what the doctors do, my outlook will be hopeless. This is an emergency! Why can't we do it tomorrow, Saturday? Hospitals should not close down for the weekends. Just this morning on the radio I heard a hospital advertising mammograms and the importance of early cancer detection. Now I'm in the doctor's hands, why this delay? Doctors preach early detection, but they must have forgotten what they preach.

I know the dean, I know the president of the medical school, maybe I should call them. If I were a millionaire or the governor, maybe that would break the logjam.

But I said nothing because I knew from experience that disturbing a well-oiled machine could result in disaster. Going out of turn increased the risk of errors; being operated on in the evening or on the weekend meant calling in a special team that was not as well coordinated as the regular team. I thought, I understand this, but how can patients understand it, and what goes through their minds at times like this?

It was late in the morning by the time I left Dr. DuVall's office. I rushed to the laboratory to get there before noon so I wouldn't have to wait through the lunch hour. But no one realized I was a physician. I used to be one of the bosses here. Now no one in the laboratory knew me. I was given a number and told to wait. Then I heard someone shout, "Don't you know who this is? This is Dr. Rosenbaum!" A big, bearded buy gave me a bear hug, and I recognized him as one of my former patients in the arthritis clinic. The technicians took me out of turn. I was getting the proper respect.

It wasn't until after dinner that night that I sat down to appraise my situation. The diagnosis was right. I had cancer. It was obviously inoperable; the doctor had told me he wanted to use X-ray treatment. I wondered how long I had to live and if I would have much pain.

"Think positive," I said to myself, and I proceeded to add up my assets. First of all, I have always said that death is not a tragedy if it occurs in sequence. That was true for me. My children were grown and on their own, but more important, I was first, none of my children had preceded me.

I had had forty-three years of a happy marriage. Not many people could say that.

Suddenly money was unimportant. I didn't have to worry about the nuclear holocaust or ecology. Nothing in the world is constant. We are part of a vast tissue that is constantly changing. Even the earth itself is in a constant state of evolution. My grandparents and my parents had already traveled the road. . . .

I couldn't sleep that night. I kept getting up, going to the bathroom, rummaging through drawers looking for samples of sleeping pills. In recent years I had seldom prescribed sleeping pills, partly because I had seen too much addiction, partly because of an experience I had had in the early days of my practice.

Will Jayson and I were both young internists with common goals. One day Will confided that his marriage was in trouble because he was unable to control his working hours. He asked how I handled the problem and I told him, "No matter how busy I am, I always come home for dinner with my family. If I have to go on a house call, I pack Dee and the kids in the station wagon and they go along for an ice cream. On Sundays I take all the boys with me on rounds. The administrator and the nurses give them some candy, and patients love to see them."

Shortly after that talk, Will and his wife were divorced. We went our separate ways, until one day the hospital administrator advised me that Will was addicted to narcotics.

"You're chief of medicine," the administrator said. "The responsibility for monitoring Jayson is yours."

It was agreed that I would review Dr. Jayson's hospital orders and that they would not be obeyed until I had countersigned them. Furthermore, I would visit his hospital patients daily. But I didn't ask who was monitoring his office practice, and in time Will's license to practice medicine was suspended.

I inherited some of his patients. Among them was Mildred Sure, a delightful woman who had a small acreage and often brought me garden-fresh vegetables, homemade jams, and, in the fall, armsful of chrysanthemums. I cared for her for many years. Shortly before she died she told me, "When I was Dr. Jayson's patient in the hospital, I was flattered that you came to see me every day. At the time, I thought you were coming for my benefit; it wasn't until later that I learned that Dr. Jayson was on drugs. You never told me. You were protecting him, not me.''

The problem of the impaired physician is even worse today. It has been estimated that 2 percent of physicians have addiction problems. Knowing what I know now, I would be more concerned with protecting the public than the physician.

I resisted taking the sleeping pills and fell into a fitful sleep. Then I had a dream in which my mother was telling Dee how to care for me. "Give him oatmeal," she advised. "Give him only pure oatmeal that has been cooked for three hours in a double boiler. Be sure he is kept warm and tucked in at night and let him have his way.''

I awoke startled. My mother had been gone three years, but I understood. At seventy years of age, I still wanted my mother at my side to nurse me. She had always regretted that she had not been educated as a doctor, but her lack of formal training did not deter her from nursing family, friends, and neighbors. Once she undertook a patient's care, she never left that person's side. In those days, survival depended more on nursing care than on the doctor's orders, and my mother was a devoted nurse. She neglected her own eating and sleeping. She was not frightened by the risk of catching the disease nor deterred by fatigue. When the patient went to the hospital, she insisted on accompanying him or her. Once ensconced in the hospital, she never left the bedside. If the hospital permitted it, she slept on a cot in the room. If not, she slept on a chair in the hallway. She monitored the doctor's orders, the diets, the nursing care, and the patient.

Many doctors and nurses are disturbed by such meddlesome family members, and at times I felt embarrassed by my mother's interference. I thought that she was overreacting and being too motherly. But today I know that she was right. Hospital mistakes are common in spite of all precautions. It is not unusual for errors in medication, diet, and procedures to occur. When I have personally discovered such errors, I have angrily corrected them. When patients have called my attention to it, I have always investigated the problem. But there has been a part of me that resented it. After all, we are the professionals and do not want our image to be tarnished or our expertise questioned.

It was when my dad had a prostatectomy that my attitude changed. I knew that my mother and the patients were right. My dad had his operation when he was ninety. Although she was eighty-six, my mother insisted on staying the night with him in his room in the hospital. During the night, the nurse changed the numerous tubes and fluid bottles that were connected to Dad without even bothering to turn on the lights. As soon as the nurse left the room, my mother examined the apparatus and found that working in the dark, the nurse had inadvertently disconnected the equipment. It was not functioning. Had the situation gone undetected, my father would not have survived the night. Such situations are not common, but they do occur. Nurses are overworked. Now that hospitals are becoming more profit-oriented and hiring even fewer nurses, such errors will become more common. Physicians worry about this, but I don't know what we are going to do. The situation has to be corrected before there are too many serious errors.

Saturday morning I awoke unrefreshed and reappraised my situation. I am not a cancer specialist, I am a rheumatologist. I have always found treating cancer patients emotionally exhausting because I shared the burden with the patient and the family. When a new medical specialty, oncology, developed, I was relieved to refer cancer patients to the specialists. Now that I thought about it, in recent years, not all the patients I referred to oncologists had died. Many cases that I had felt were hopeless were surviving.

Even in my own family, we've come through a couple of bouts with the disease and defeated it. When my wife, Dee, was in her late forties, a small cancer was discovered in her uterus and removed. During the course of her annual examination a few years later, her physician suggested that she participate in a mammogram study.

When Dee discussed the idea with me, I answered, "I don't know. My motto is, Be neither the first nor the last to try something new." After a month I relented, and Dee had a mammogram. It showed a few pinhead calcium spots in one breast but no lumps. Two doctors agreed that the mammogram was normal, but a third one insisted that she should have a breast biopsy. It showed an early cancer. I was in the surgical suite when the pathologist pronounced the dreaded word "malignant," and I was stunned. I stumbled to the doctors' lounge and sat by myself and wondered, What will I do now? Our sons are grown. Kenny, the youngest, has just left for Yale. We are alone. Who will be there when I get up? Who will be there when I come home from the office? Who will be there to hold on to at night when I need refuge from the day's frustrations? But we survived that trauma. Dee had a mastectomy, and fourteen years later, she is well.

If my own disease is not too far advanced, I have a chance, I thought. But after all, I knew that the cancer had been present since November. It was now July, a long delay—a delay that might have been avoided if the examination had been done in a more up-to-date manner and if I had been exercising the same detached judgment in my own case that I would have with a patient. As a patient, my judgment had been impaired.

Sunday night I had a second dream. This time I was a little boy playing in the yard. I could see my childhood home. My mother was baking a cake and my father was reading a newspaper. My grandparents, all four of them, came for a visit. Long-gone uncles and aunts came. All of them hugged and kissed me. I was a little boy, and I was very happy.

The dream did not alarm me because I'd heard of something very like it before. For its size, Portland has a large population of Chinese, Japanese, Koreans, and Vietnamese. The Chinese were brought in to do the heavy work of the railroad construction crews. When the railroads were finished and their labor was no longer needed, restrictive immigration laws were passed to keep out the Asians, and the Chinese then had to come in surreptitiously. The new immigrants worked for almost nothing in the laundries and restaurants. They were afraid to go out on the streets for fear of being accosted by Immigration officials, so they rarely left their place of employment. They worked, ate, and slept in one place. They could not escape because they could not understand the culture and did not learn the language.

One of these workers came to me as a patient in 1950. He was accompanied by three buddies who were supposed to act as interpreters, but in truth none of them could speak English. I liked them, I had empathy with them because of my own family's history, and somehow I understood what they needed and I helped. From then on, I became a friend of and physician for many of the Chinese in Portland. I attended their weddings, their birthday celebrations, and their funerals.

When this particular patient became ill, because he had no family, I put him in a nursing home, and I am sorry to say that three months passed before I found the time to call on him.

He greeted me reproachfully. "You forgot me."

"I can't deny it," I said. "Were you lonesome?"

"No, I had visitors every night."

He's senile, I thought.

"They come every night, people long since dead . . . my father, my mother, my childhood friends from the village. They come every night and talk to me."

"Does it frighten you?"

"Not at all," he assured me. "They are ghosts who come to comfort me. I feel good in their presence."

At the time it happened, I thought: a Chinese belief, ancestor worship. Imagine seeing ghosts at night and enjoying it! But when I had my dream, I understood what the old gentleman had said to me. He was chiding me for having neglected him, and so he turned to his ancestors. I felt guilty for my neglect. I was brought up close to my grandparents, and I had empathy for the aged. When I first started practice, I paid special attention to them. If they were alone and in nursing homes, I visited them at least once a week. I had been appointed by the governor to the Oregon Council on Aging. I had been elected as a delegate to a White House conference on aging. Then, as my practice grew and I became busier, my visits to the nursing homes became less frequent. Now that I was a patient and facing chronic infirmity, I understood better how those elderly people felt. What if I, too, were to end up in a nursing home? I knew now that I must go back to my old ways and visit patients in nursing homes at least once a week.

I awoke Tuesday morning with a tight feeling in my belly. I knew that sensation. It was the way I had felt in World War II when I boarded a ship for an invasion. When I graduated from medical school, I accepted a commission as a first lieutenant in the Army Medical Corps Reserves. Both sets of grandparents had imbued me with a strong sense of patriotism. They constantly reminded me of what had happened to our family; they had come to America with nothing, and here they found citizenship, the right to vote, the right to own property. They had a house and garden, food to eat, and a synagogue in which to worship God. Their children were becoming doctors, lawyers, and successful businessmen. This never could have been under the czar. America was paradise, and paradise was worth dying for. I could not at that time conceive of not serving if the United States went to war, nor could I believe that America would ever be involved in an unjust war; in those days I firmly adhered to the precept, "My country, right or wrong." In 1938, with no military training at all, I accepted a commission as a first lieutenant in the army reserves.

In 1941, before Pearl Harbor, while I was still in training in internal medicine at the Mayo Clinic, my fellowship
was interrupted by orders to active duty. After the war
began, I was with the first American troops sent to Great
Britain, and from there I participated in the invasion of
North Africa, the African campaign, and the invasion of
Sicily. After that, I returned to England to participate in
the D-Day invasion of Normandy. I was in the army for
five years, two and a half of them overseas.

I started as a first lieutenant; I was discharged as a major, but I never learned the "courage" of an officer. When
I went over a ship's side for an invasion, what I felt was
terror, sheer terror. What was going to happen was unpredictable, and there was nothing I could do but submit to
my fate. But this time, I told myself, it's not the army. At
least my wife will be at my side, I'll have clean sheets,
I'll be able to shower, and even if I can't eat, the food
will smell good.

I insisted on driving the car to the hospital myself. I
needed to be in command. Being in the medical school
gave me no sense of security. I have known governors and
senators to die of cancer. Even worse, doctors, chiefs of
medicine and surgery, had died in this hospital. In this
institution I was a full professor, a former division chief,
but now no one knew me. Again I had to go through the
admissions process like anyone else. The clerk asked the
same questions, and again I understood their purpose.
They would have been ordinary in ordinary circumstances,
but I saw that they were gruesome when the patient might
have a terminal illness.

In recent years the state legislature had been ruthless in
slashing the medical school budget. Now the hospital was
stark; not even a rug was on the floor. My room was like
a monk's cell—small, bare, with off-white walls, a narrow
steel bed, and barely enough room for one hard visitor's
chair. There were no residents or students on the floor and
only one nurse at the nurse's station.

I remembered in years past working on this same floor

when it was alive and bustling. In those days its rooms were full of patients from all over the state who presented difficult diagnostic problems. The halls were buzzing with students, teachers, and residents grappling with problems. Now that money was scarce, the floor had to support itself economically. It was no longer a great diagnostic and teaching center; it was a day surgery floor. I wondered who was caring for the difficult patients now. I vowed that if I survived and was able to talk again, I would visit the state capitol to give the politicians in the legislature hell. . . . And then I stopped, a patient again, and prayed that their penuriousness had not jeopardized my own care.

Once again the indignity of the nurse taking all my clothes away, tying a too-short apron around my neck, and having me sign the fine-printed release form. Once more I had to wait four hours until the surgical suite was ready for me.

The resident came in, took my history, listened to my heart and lungs, felt my neck and belly, and asked if I needed a sedative. "No," I told him. He smiled and left. Now the anesthesiologist came in and asked the same questions the resident had—Did I smoke? Did I drink? Was I allergic?—and he listened to my heart and lungs. I thought to myself, "Boy, they do a fast, lousy physical examination. I'm just a number. All they're doing is going through the motions. In case I die under anesthesia, they can prove to the lawyers in a malpractice suit that they had examined me. That's all this quick job is accomplishing."

As the morning wore on and I became more apprehensive, I regretted that I had refused a preoperative sedative. I began to have memories of my childhood and wondered if this is what they mean when they say that your past life rolls before your eyes just before death. I particularly recalled an incident that had occurred when I was five or six years old, in Omaha. At that time, we lived in what used to be a Jewish neighborhood where everybody knew everyone else. The houses were wood frame and stood on individual lots. The lawns were ill kept, but the streets were clean and the porches were swept. Around the corner were the neighborhood stores. On Thursdays I would accompany my grandmother to shop for the Sabbath meal. The first stop was the grocery; there was fish to buy. Omaha offered us only river fish, buffalo, and carp; the catfish was forbidden. There was no true refrigeration, and my grandmother would never accept a dead fish on ice. The grocery had a large concrete tank with live fish swimming in it. The housewife would point to the fish she wanted, and the grocer would clean it in front of her and wrap it in an old newspaper. Then she would inspect the barrels of schmaltz herring, pickles, and sauerkraut and look in the bins of oatmeal and kasha.

Next door was the butcher store. It smelled of spices from the corned beef, and there was sawdust on the floor. The butcher was fat, and his belly stretched his bloodstained white apron. There were pens with live fowl. Grandma selected the chicken she wanted, felt it to be sure it was fat enough, then handed it to the butcher and accompanied him to the back room, where she watched him ritually slaughter it according to Jewish law. Then she had a choice of either plucking the feathers herself or paying the shop boy a nickel to do it. To have the boy do it would be ostentatious. Besides, a nickel would buy meat for another meal, a soupbone, some lung or liver or spleen. My grandmother always plucked her own chicken, as most women did.

Next door was the bakery. During the week it offered only rye bread or a coarse black bread known as Russian pumpernickel. If you ate that, you didn't have to eat bran flakes. But on weekends, there was no black bread, only challah, the fine egg bread with braided top. Grandma always ordered two loaves fresh baked for Friday.

But this Thursday Grandma didn't feel well, and it was my mother who had to make the shopping rounds. On Friday morning my grandmother was still ill, and by Friday afternoon an ambulance came to take her away to the hospital. It was a neighborhood event. How the news spread so fast I'll never know, but I suspect it was the gossip in the butcher shop. Her friends were all there when she was wheeled on a cart from the house to the ambulance. They all gathered around her and wailed as she was lifted into the car to be taken to the hospital.

It was my grandfather's custom to go to the synagogue on Friday and seek a stranger to seat at our table for the festive dinner. But this Friday was different. There was no stranger and no grandmother. After my mother set the table and lit the Sabbath candles, my grandfather said the prayer over the wine, and as we sat at our meal, I was startled to see huge tears rolling down his face and over his white beard. I had never seen him cry before. I knew he loved me because he used to hug and kiss me and toss me in the air, but I had never seen him kiss my grandmother or put his arm around her. My mother removed his soup plate and placed a plate of chicken before him. "Ess, Tata," she pleaded, "you must not desecrate the Sabbath."

"I can't," he sobbed, "they have taken her to the hospital to die."

"In Europe they go to the hospital to die, in America we go to the hospital to live," my mother assured him. And she continued, "If I had been born a boy, I would now be a doctor."

My grandfather was shocked. "Decent girls don't become doctors," he angrily told her.

At that time in my life I believed my mother: that hospitals were places to live. Now in the hospital myself, my confidence was dampened. Sometimes patients, even doctors, died in hospitals. I thought again how nice it would be if my mother were here to nurse me, but I realized that my illness would have devastated her. I once heard her say to a friend, "When my boys were overseas in the war I prayed to God, and I promised Him that if my sons returned unharmed, I would never again ask anything of Him. Now that they are home and well, I can't keep my promise. I still worry about them and keep asking God to give them even more."

My mother died when I was sixty-seven. When I cried at her funeral, I apologized to the rabbi. "I have no right to cry," I said. "How many people can have their mother when they're in their late sixties?" And the rabbi answered, "You have a right to cry for your mother even if you're a hundred."

I was now seventy. I had problems, and I wanted my mother.

Finally the nurse rolled a cart into the room. "They're ready," she said. I was transferred to the gurney. Because I was cold, they covered me with a blanket, and the cart started to roll. All I could see were the lights in the ceiling and the doors automatically opening and closing. We went through the last set of doors, and I was looking into the anesthetist's face. I felt one little stick, and then I was asleep.

When I awoke I was still looking into the anesthetist's face. He was checking my pulse. "What did they find?" I asked. "I don't know," he said. "I was too busy giving the anesthesia."

I knew he was lying. Good news is not withheld. They wheeled me back to the hospital floor. I could see Dee walking toward me, and I knew from the look on her face what the decision was. "It's malignant," she said.

They lifted me off the cart onto the bed. Neither of us said anything. I was still too drowsy from the anesthesia to feel the impact of the diagnosis.

Late in the day the doctor came. "The biopsy was positive," he said. "Do you want a second opinion?"

"No," I said, "you're already my second and third opinions. But how are you going to treat me?"

"Xray."

"Why not surgery? Let's get rid of it."

"If I have to operate," he explained, "you will lose your voice because I'll remove the cords, and because of the location of the lesion I may have to put in a permanent tracheotomy. You have an eighty-five percent chance of cure with X ray."

"You know how old I am?"

"Of course."

"Okay. I'm old enough to know. Tell me everything. Don't keep anything from me." That was to impress the doctor and Dee with how brave I was. The truth was that if I really wanted to know everything, all I had to do was to walk across the street to the library and read the medical literature.

"Good. That will make it easier for both of us. Who would you like to be in charge of the X-ray therapy?"

"I don't know," I answered. "Why do you ask?"

"Well," he answered, "I thought you might have a friend who is a radiologist."

"I have confidence in the radiologists in town. They have treated my patients well, but I would rather that you make the choice."

I had friends who were radiologists, but I had already suffered twice by going to friends and turning my care over to them. I had avoided exercising my own judgment, but isn't that what patients are supposed to do? Isn't that what I've always required of my own patients? That they trust me to make the medical decisions? I felt my head spinning as I realized that my only choice was to go to the best doctor that could be found.

"I recommend Dr. Reed to you," my doctor was saying. "He's the best X-ray therapist in the northwest."

"The best in the Northwest? Man, I don't want the best in the northwest. I want the best in the world."

"I don't know," he answered. "Maybe Reed is the best in the world."

"Okay, I'll take your word for it. Make an appointment for me to see him."

"Your appointment's tomorrow. Before Reed sees you, you'll need a CAT scan of your neck." He handed me the appointment slips.

"How could you have made these appointments for me before I consented?"

"I knew that you had learned your lesson," he an-

swered. "I expected you to leave the choice up to me.
Any other questions?"

"No."

"Good. You can go home."

Go home? I thought. They gave me a general anesthetic,
they cut my throat, and they haven't even given me a drink.
Now they're sending me home? What if I can't swallow?
What if I start to bleed? What if my throat swells in the
middle of the night and I can't catch my breath? Would I
send someone I was treating home so fast? Was I right to
put my fate in this man's hands?

Well, at least I knew the reason for the rapid discharge.
Medicare and the insurance carriers have set a fixed fee.
Whether I stay two hours or ten days in the hospital, it
will receive the same amount of money. The faster I'm
out, the less it costs them.

Because I hated the sterility of the small room and the
feeling of being in the hospital and because, like other
sick and worried people, I had begun to obey my doctor,
I didn't object. I meekly turned to Dee and asked her to
put my things into the suitcase. Then I turned to the doctor. "I do have one more question," I said. "What caused
this?"

"It occurs in heavy smokers and heavy drinkers."

"That's not me," I answered. "I neither smoke nor
drink."

He didn't reply; only turned on his heel and walked out.
A typical doctor, I thought; it's impossible for him to say,
"I don't know."

It has taken me years to utter those words. From the
first day of medical school, young doctors understand that
they can never learn it all, yet they are constantly questioned and tested and expected to give answers. From day
one they are conditioned never to say, "I don't know."
There are many diseases of unknown cause and for which
there is no treatment, yet there are endless medical papers
and medical texts discussing their causes and therapy.
When I wrote a text on rheumatic diseases, I had to write

a section on scleroderma, and I was tempted to describe it in only one sentence: "Scleroderma: we don't know the cause and we don't have the treatment." But if I had done that, no publisher would issue my book and no doctors would buy it, so I wrote that chapter full of theory.

It was one of my patients, Alicia Bloom, who taught me my lesson on this subject. In her eighties, Mrs. Bloom had a kindly face and a warm smile, and when she talked, her sweetness shone through. She was not a complainer, and when she mentioned pain and swelling in her right knee, I knew there was trouble. When I told her that she had arthritis, she asked me what had caused it. I said, "You've worked hard all your life, raised your children, scrubbed floors, climbed stairs, and cared for your house. You knee is worn out."

"That's very funny," she replied. "My right knee has arthritis. My left knee is perfect. You say the arthritis is due to wear and tear, but both knees were born at the same time."

I laughed with Mrs. Bloom as if we were sharing a joke, but I would have done better to admit that nobody really knows why one knee can be arthritic and the other not— or why someone like me, a nonsmoker and a nondrinker, gets cancer of the larynx.

For the first time since I had suspected the diagnosis, I felt some relief because now I was living with certainty, not indecision. Events were proceeding in a way that I had advised patients they would. When patients would ask, "Should I get a divorce? Should I change my job? Should I do this or that?" my answer usually was, "I can't advise you how to live your life, but I'd make a firm decision as soon as possible. The quicker you reach that decision, the quicker the tension will disappear."

As soon as we were settled at home, Dee called the office to tell them the bad news. We practice as a small family group; I as a general internist and rheumatologist, my brother, Bill, as a general surgeon, and two of our sons, Richard and Robert, as neurologists. There was one outsider, Dr. John, a general internist who had been associated with us for thirty years. Upset as I was with my illness, I still worried about the office. Over the years I had never taken a long vacation or been away many weekends. Who else but I could take care of my patients? Yet the practice had grown beyond my capacity. Patients had to wait too long to see me, and I often felt that I didn't have time to sit back and think. At my age, I was busier than I had ever been in my life. We had recently hired a new associate, but she wasn't due to join us for another three months. My whole practice load would fall on Dr. John, but he already had all he could do to care for his own patients. I was worried. I had been imbued by my mother, my training, and my own compulsiveness: "The sick patient comes first." But what happens to the quality of care when everything's done in a rush, when diagnosis is made on the fly—as it probably had been earlier in my own case?

That evening, my eldest son, Richard, stopped on his way home from our office. Both of us believed that the time for parting had come. I should have offered him some final words of wisdom or maybe a parental blessing. Instead we played the charade that cancer patients and their families frequently play.

"What shall we do about your office appointments?" he asked.

"Well, my X-ray treatment should take about a month, so sign me out for thirty days."

"Maybe we should make it six weeks to give you a little rest."

"Okay," I agreed. "Now go home and enjoy your family."

I didn't want him to stay too long, for I feared I would cry. He rose to leave. Neither of us could keep the tears from our eyes, but we said nothing more; fathers and sons.

Later in the evening my number two son, Jimmy, called from San Francisco. By then I was more composed.

"Dad," he assured me, "I spent the entire afternoon in the library reviewing the literature. The outlook for cancer of the vocal cord treated by Xray is good."

That may be true, I thought, but good wasn't enough. What does good mean? One year? Six months? Freedom from pain?

"Thanks, Jim," I said. "I know you're right." I did not say to him that I had had trouble for at least six months. The delay had been too long.

I still had not made my adjustment. Any discussion of my illness, as well meant as it was, reinforced in my mind the thought that my time was short.

The next call came from number three son, Howard, the psychiatrist. "How are you taking it, Dad?" he asked.

I wasn't ready to reveal my psyche to him. After all, I was the father; he was the son. So I did what psychiatrists do.

"How should I take it?" I asked, avoiding discussion of the painful subject.

The fourth son, lawyer Kenny, called from Washington. "Dad, you have a good malpractice suit," he advised.

I knew he was right. There had been a six-month delay in diagnosis. That could be fatal. The earlier the diagnosis, the better the chance for remission or cure. But in order for there to be malpractice, there has to be some damage. If I admitted that there was malpractice, that meant that my prognosis was poor because of the delay. I couldn't do it at that time, so I said to Kenny, "Forget it. I'm going to be cured." But I didn't believe it.

My brother, Bill, stopped by on his way home from the office. He brought with him a get-well card with caring notes from all the office personnel. Then he told me that Winifred, our office manager, had burst into tears when she heard the news. I was moved, but I suppressed my tears and only said, "Bill, you know how girls are." Then I said, "You never really approved of Al Cade, did you?"

"No."

"Why not?"

"Technically he's good, but somehow or other I always felt that he was too business-oriented."

"How can you say that? None of us works for peanuts. Remember when we were kids in Omaha, how Mom always held up Dr. Drummond as an example to us? He was an eye specialist who never sent a patient a bill. Whatever the patient voluntarily brought in was okay with him. The amazing thing is that he was able to make a living. He never got rich, it was during the Depression, but somehow or other he got along."

"We've done our share," Bill said. "You donate time to the medical school, we have our share of free patients, and we never pressed a patient for payment." Then Bill said quietly, "Maybe you should have gotten a second opinion earlier."

"Yeah, then whose opinion do you follow?" I asked. "Remember when you advised a woman to have a hysterectomy and as she walked down the hall to leave she told you she wanted a second opinion. You took her by the hand, led her into another room in our office, and said, "I'll give you a second opinion, don't have an operation.' "

"That's right," Bill said, "how do you know which opinion is right? Gill Holm has been in practice as long as we have. Now that his granddaughter has multiple sclerosis and isn't getting any better, he's taking her to the fifth doctor. And remember Red Conley, who taught eye, ear, nose, and throat when we were in school? He always said, 'When I'm called in consultation, I always ask what the other consultant advised. If he advised hot packs, I advise cold packs.' "

I wasn't laughing. In fact, I was getting angry. "It's a joke when you're not the patient. It's tragic when you're the one who's sick. I should have gotten another doctor as soon as I was told to use penicillin for hoarseness. Maybe a patient wouldn't know that, but I should have."

Wednesday was the day of decision. The scheduled tests would determine whether or not I was treatable. I went to the Xray department with my little slips, one for a CAT scan, one for a chest X ray. The chest X ray was to determine whether the cancer had spread to the lymph nodes in my chest. The CAT scan consisted of multiple X rays taken and scrutinized by computer, a more certain way to determine the extent of the cancer. If the lymph nodes showed involvement, my outlook was poor. I found myself wishing that we didn't have modern, sophisticated techniques; I didn't really want to know. About my patients—all the information I could get. About myself—just so much.

The chest X ray was routine, like having your photo taken, but the CAT scan was an hour-long procedure. To prepare for it the technician started an intravenous on me, a slow drip of a contrast material to help demonstrate the lymph glands in the neck. I knew that there was iodine in the material and that occasionally a patient allergic to the iodine could have a severe reaction, even die. I hoped that there was a good emergency team standing by. For one hour I lay rigid while the intravenous dripped, dripped, dripped and the machine rotated and clicked, clicked, clicked. I didn't dare move; a blur could be misinterpreted or misread as an enlarged node.

The X rays and CAT scan were all done in the diagnostic X-ray department. It was now almost eleven o'clock, and I had to go to my appointment in the Xray therapy department on a different floor. As I got off the elevator the signs all pointed to X-ray therapy, and as I entered the waiting room my experienced eye told me that all the patients waiting had cancer.

When hospitals first introduced special floors for the exclusive treatment of cancer patients, I resented it. I felt it was wrong. I believed that was rubbing it in. But now I found that I actually felt better knowing that I was on a floor with other cancer patients with similar problems.

I had to wait fifteen minutes in the reception room, but it seemed like an hour. What would Dr. Reed tell me? Would he consider me treatable? Finally the receptionist escorted me into a tiny examining room. First the resident came and took my history again. I sat impatiently wondering how many times I would have to tell my life story. It was as if I had to make that payment every time I got some service performed. Finally, after he'd taken the information he already had in the chart from the hospital, I gathered my courage to ask him if the reports on my chest X ray and on my CAT scan had arrived. "I looked at the chest X ray myself," he said. "That's negative. The CAT scan won't be ready for twenty-four hours."

The report of a normal X ray didn't satisfy me. The uninitiated think that X rays are a perfect tool, but I knew better. X rays are black-and-white shadows subject to interpretation. I have known X rays to be read as normal and months later, when the patient was discovered to have a disease, to be reread as abnormal. Early in my career I learned not to rely completely on X-ray reports from a roly-poly radiologist whose cigar stank up the X-ray darkrooms. He thought he was infallible and convinced the attending surgeon that a shadow in the colon was a malignant tumor. The surgeon removed a normal colon in which there was no tumor; it was stool they both had seen.

Since then, the rule in our office was that every X ray must be read by at least two doctors. In spite of that precaution, once in a while a film would be misread, a diagnosis missed.

Dr. Reed, the radiotherapist, is in his middle fifties, with a thick head of hair and a mustache. When he came in to see me, he didn't act nationally famous or like the best in the world or even the northwest. But then he did something that comforted me. He smiled. He was the first doctor who had done that. I knew that he was only being pleasant, but it gave me some hope. I realized that I was looking for any sign that everything was all right. Like a child—or a patient.

As the first doctors had done, Dr. Reed looked into my throat with mirrors and said, "I can't see anything. It looks normal."

I was shocked at the technique this highly recommended specialist was using, but before I could speak, the resident said, "You can't see anything because Dr. DuVall told me it's underneath the cord. You can only see it with a fiberoptic nasopharyngoscope."

Dr. Reed asked for a nasopharyngoscope. The resident again anesthetized my nose and throat, and it was he who passed the instrument through my nose into my larynx. Then he gave it to Dr. Reed, who said, "I can't see a thing." And I asked myself a question that I, a physician, could not answer: Is it better to see an old man who has a lot of experience but is unacquainted with the latest techniques or to see a young man who is up on the latest techniques but has had no experience?

After completing the exam, Dr. Reed looked at me. He was not smiling now. "I think that you have about an eighty-five percent chance of cure with X-ray therapy, and I would recommend that as the best way to go."

"What about chemotherapy?"

"Useless."

I felt relieved. I had seen too many patients suffer from nausea, vomiting, and hair loss as a result of chemotherapy. The results of chemotherapy were always so questionable, I was glad to escape the ordeal. "What if my glands are involved?" I asked.

"I won't treat you."

"I have no choice?"

"I don't think so," Dr. Reed replied. "It will take about thirty treatments. Your first visit will take an hour because we'll spend time positioning you on the table, locating the exact position of the lesion, and getting measurements on the machine. Every visit after that, you'll be put on the same spot on the table, and the machine will be positioned in the same place so that we can focus on the lesion and avoid treating healthy tissue."

"Will I be sick?"

"Usually not. Some people get nauseated by X ray. Some complain of a great deal of fatigue. You will, though, probably have a very sore throat and difficulty in swallowing."

"Any other risks?"

"Well," he said, "occasionally some patients will develop a necrosis of the throat cartilage."

"What happens then?" I asked.

"They have to have it removed and have a tracheotomy. But," he added reassuringly, "that's never happened to me." Then he turned to the resident. "Do you have any comments?"

"How do you determine the dosage?" asked the resident. And Dr. Reed answered, "It will all be done by computer."

I thought to myself what computer programmers always say: "Garbage in, garbage out." I hoped this computer was better than the one my bank used.

As Dee and I drove home I realized that Dr. Reed had not followed the letter of the law, as he had not discussed any alternative treatments nor had he really discussed all the risks of radiation therapy. From my own experience I knew that it was dangerous. I knew that severe, untreatable skin burns could result. I knew that the esophagus could become inflamed so that I wouldn't be able to swallow or to eat. I knew that I could develop skin cancer. I knew that I would be more prone to develop cancer elsewhere after this treatment. I knew that X-ray overdosage could result in death. And I was sure there were a lot of side effects that I did not know of. Why hadn't the doctor discussed these problems with me and my wife?

At a recent medical malpractice seminar I had attended, an attorney had emphasized how important it was to advise the patient of all the risks. Surely Dr. Reed was aware of all that.

Of course the policy is sometimes very difficult for the patient. A friend of mine who took his dying son to a national cancer center for treatment told me that the ordeal of going through the informed consent was worse than his son's treatment. As he described it, the physician at the cancer center slowly read to them a list of all the possible side effects of the treatment, and every five minutes she would stop and ask, "Do you understand?"

My friend said, "As she read the gruesome possibilities, I could only say to myself, this can't happen to us. After an hour of listening to the horrible possibilities, I could no longer hear what she was saying, but it took another half hour of detailed explanations before she finally finished. My son, Barry, and I were numb, and we signed a paper. To this day I don't know what it said."

I have wrestled with this problem in my practice. I know of no effective treatment that is innocuous. In certain circumstances, any drug can cause death. Yet the human psyche must be reckoned with. If a patient fears the drug, the psychotherapeutic effects are lost, and even worse, the patient probably doesn't take it. I have resolved the problem in my practice by saying, "The law and the threat of malpractice be damned; I'll do what is best for my patient and let the chips fall where they may."

I try to evaluate my patients individually and tell them only what I think they can handle. Then I conclude the interview with, "Is there anything else you would like to know?" Occasionally a patient responds, "I want to know the worst." In those cases I am forced to tell the worst. That type of patient appears to exhibit extraordinary bravery, but, I've noticed, seldom cooperates fully in the treatment. Perhaps they have given up because their prognosis is so poor. In my own case, on the other hand, I'd avoided facing what was wrong with me and had contributed to the delay in my treatment.

At home that evening, I had another important problem to grapple with. Unlike most patients, I knew many of the risks of treatment the doctors had avoided mentioning. Always, there is the rare risk of an unexpectedly adverse reaction to therapy. In my practice I would protect most of my patients against worrying about remote, unlikely complications, but because I was a doctor and knew too much, there was no one to protect me. What did I want to do? If I started my X-ray treatment, there would be no turning back. I had to decide now whether I wanted a second opinion. Dr. DuVall had made it simple for me. He had asked if I did, and I admired him for the question. It had taken me years to reach that point in myself.

Doctors are competitive. It starts in college. There were, for a long time, three applicants for every opening in medical school. Unless you were on top of the heap, you didn't get in. In medical school, you are constantly examined. You are always aware of your class standing, for it will determine the quality of your residency, and how you do in your residency will determine the opportunities for practice. Competition carries over to the second opinion; to agree with the first doctor does not add stature. Some doctors may give a contrary opinion only to increase their own standing.

A patient I was treating for hypertension told me that she had consulted a doctor in California while on vacation. He had changed her medication and advised her, "The doctors in Oregon aren't as up to date as we are in California, so I'm changing your prescription." I had prescribed Hydrodiuril. He changed her prescription to Esidrix. He hadn't changed her medicine at all. The two drugs are exactly the same. The only difference was in the brand names.

To voluntarily suggest a second opinion, a doctor has to feel secure. I had reached that point in my own practice and was comfortable with second opinions; in fact, they lessened my own responsibility. But as to my own case, I wondered why I had been so foolish. Why had I waited so long to see DuVall? In spite of all the excuses I had made to myself, I knew the reason. I had acted like many of my patients had, accepting the diagnosis to avoid facing something else.

I liked Kitty Grant from the very first visit because of a remark calculated to seduce any doctor. "I know you're the best doctor in the world," she said. "That's why I'm here, so that you can help my arthritis. I've already been to six doctors. You're my last hope.''

I took her history and was surprised by the physical examination. She did not have arthritis, she had multiple sclerosis. No question about that.

How do you tell an unsuspecting patient bad news? As gently as I could I told her, and she wasn't even upset.

''Did you suspect the diagnosis?'' I asked.

''Well, not exactly. The first doctor I went to told me that.''

''And the next five doctors?''

''They all treated me for arthritis or something like that.''

''Why did you leave the first doctor?''

''I didn't like his diagnosis.''

In my case, the first two doctors had told me what I wanted to hear, ''No cancer.'' Why look elsewhere?

I knew about the great cancer centers in America: Sloan-Kettering, the Mayo Clinic, the National Institutes of Health, Stanford, Houston, and, even closer to home, Seattle. I had connections, and knew doctors at all those institutions. At any one of those places, I would have been welcomed with open arms. But I made my decision as any other patient would have; I liked my own doctors, and I wanted to be treated where I was most comfortable. I wanted to be close to my family during my time of crisis. I elected to be treated in Portland. If I was going to die, I wanted to die at home.

It had been a long day, but I approached bedtime that evening with some equanimity. I had made my decisions. I had determined to act like a mature adult. For most of my life I had been in command; now, for the first time, my destiny was in other hands. I had finally accepted that. I knew the problems, I knew the things that could go wrong, but the fact is, I told myself, people in my profession know what they're doing. If they don't, if you can't trust yourself to them, then what's my whole life been about?

* * *

In bed I snuggled up close to Dee and held her tight. I didn't anticipate being able to do that much longer. Even if I survived my illness, I expected to be sick from the Xray treatment.

I thought about a day a few years before, when my dad was ninety and my mother was eighty-six. Mom developed a fever, and Dad asked, "What's the matter with Bessie?"

"She's got a fever, Pop. She probably has the flu."

"Is it contagious?"

"Probably."

"Then maybe I shouldn't sleep with her tonight?"

"Right," I answered.

"Eddie," he said, and he was very serious, "you better talk to her and explain it to her. She'll never consent to my sleeping in another bed."

I felt good when I thought of that story and how lucky my parents had been to sleep happily together every night for sixty-six years. And then I thought to myself: I won't be that lucky; it doesn't look like I'm going to make it. Tomorrow my life changes.

THE TREATMENT

TREATMENT DAY ONE

Today I will start X-ray therapy. After so many years as a doctor, one would think I would understand and know what to expect, but I really don't. I've referred many patients for radiation treatment, but prescribing is different than receiving.

I am worried. In my case, it has taken six months and three consultations to make what should have been an easy diagnosis. Never before have I realized how agonizing the wait is for the patient. As a doctor making a diagnosis, I followed routine steps with each patient. First the history, then the examination, then the laboratory tests, and then the X rays. Then, if the answer was not apparent, more laboratory tests, more X rays, and then consultations. It all took time. The subject waited patiently, but each delay increased the apprehension. I never knew what it was like to sit and wait and wonder; now I do.

My appointment for treatment is at ten. I arrive five minutes early, and the receptionist stops me before I enter the waiting room. I am grateful that she whisks me immediately into the treatment area. Two girls greet me by name. Obviously they have been expecting me. This is the medical school, so I know that one is a student technician and the other a trained technician. I only hope that they don't let the student do the measurements.

I understand that beginners have to learn. When I was in medical school, we were allowed on the wards when we were juniors, and we were admonished, "Look, lis-

57

ten, smell, and touch, but don't do anything else. Don't make any decisions.'' One classmate, Larry LaBelle, was touched by a patient's complaints, so he removed a bladder catheter. When that patient started to bleed, Larry's medical career ended. Over the years, to meet student demands of more hands-on experience, the rigid rules have been relaxed—I hope not too much in this department. I realize that the student needs the experience, but, as other people must have thought, why on me?

They escort me into a small, brightly lit room. In the middle is another long, narrow table, and above the table is a huge globe similar to the one that hung above the CAT scan table. Both technicians are smiling and bubbly; caring for cancer patients has apparently not depressed them. But they are young, life is ahead of them, and death is a stranger.

They ask me to remove my sweater and unbutton my shirt collar and the top two buttons. Then I step on a stool and lie down on the hard, narrow steel table. The metal is cold, and there isn't even a sheet under me. The glare of the ceiling lights forces me to half close my eyes. In some ways this helps, because it takes me away from reality.

"This will take about an hour," they tell me. "It will be a little uncomfortable, but it won't be painful. We have to exactly locate your larynx. Then we have to focus the beams on the larynx so that we will treat the same spot every time."

Now the two technicians begin a discussion of my anatomy. One says, "He's short-necked."

"Yes, we'll have to do something about it," and they slip a pillow under my neck so that it is arched.

"It won't work, too thick-necked," says the first.

"Try a size C." Under my neck they place a plastic block with a hollow which fits my neck, and my neck is further extended.

"Looks like he'll need a D."

It sounds like they're fitting me for bra cups.

"Head's okay," one says.

"Now for the knees," the other responds.

They place a hard support under my knees, bending them.

"Damn," one says. "Now his big shoulders stick up in the way."

Across my feet they place a board with a rope on each end. They hand me the ends of the rope.

"Now, pull," they order. I pull, and this forces my shoulders down. Now, finally, I am in position. There is a block of plastic under my neck so that it is stretched. I am tugging on the ropes anchored to a board against which my feet are pushing, forcing my shoulders down, and there is a support under my knees. I am lying on a hard table, a bright light is glaring in my face, and I am advised to be calm and hold steady in this position for one hour.

They explain to me that they are going to take a series of X-ray pictures to help them determine exactly where my larynx is. After that they will focus the X-ray beams on the exact spot of the larynx that is diseased. By keeping the beams narrow, they hope to strike primarily the diseased tissue itself and spare the normal tissue. To lessen the impact on the normal tissue, they will focus first on the left side and then on the right side, the beam coming to an exact point focus. In that way the normal tissue will be getting less than half the exposure that the diseased tissue is. That's their hope.

The next half hour is spent rotating the ball, snapping pictures and readjusting my head. Finally, when I think that I can pull and hold no longer, they announce, "You're in focus."

Then Dr. Reed enters the room. He doesn't say a word to me. He feels my neck, looks at the X rays and says, "Okay." Then he walks out. I am stupefied by his behavior.

The chief technician now advises me that she is going to put four permanent tattoo marks on my neck. It will tell them and future technicians where to focus the beams, and I will be marked for life. But in this way no one will ever make the mistake of giving me X-ray therapy in that particular area again. The present plan is to give the maximum amount of X ray possible without burning me. The amount will be determined by a computer. They are going to throw the dice only once. If the X-ray treatment fails, it cannot be repeated.

I want them to be on target, and so I hold as still as I possibly can. I feel a few pinpricks, and then I am marked.

Now, finally, I am ready for the first treatment.

The big eye is rotated to the left. The room lights go out. A beam of light projects from the eye and focuses on my neck. The technicians then advise me that I will be left alone. They can't be in the room. The X-ray beams are too deadly. They will be behind lead shields and will be watching me on a television screen to be sure that I don't move. With that explanation, they run out of the room. I hear a click and a whirring sound. The noise lasts exactly thirty seconds. The lights come on, and the technicians return and efficiently rotate the big eye to my right. Again the lights go out, the beam shoots from the eye to my neck, again they scurry out of the room, there's a click and a whirring. I count exactly thirty seconds.

Treatment number one is over. They help me off the table. I am a little stiff, but otherwise I haven't felt any pain.

As I drive home, I mull over the impersonal way the girls discussed my anatomy: "Thick neck, shoulders too wide." All this said as if I weren't there. It's a bad medical habit I'm familiar with, though I've never thought about it before. All my life I have heard the phrases "a senile old man, a little old lady, the crock in room 411."

When I was about ten, my mother took me to the store for my annual new suit for Rosh Hashanah, the Jewish New Year. When my mother complained that the jacket's collar didn't fit right, the salesman said, "It can't fit because his neck's too thick." My mother angrily grabbed my arm and led me out of the store. We never went to that store again, and, as far as I can remember, I put the whole thing out of my mind.

A patient of mine did that too. When Hazel Beson first come to see me, she was thirty-five, with no problems except for some extra weight: she was five feet three inches tall and weighted 155 pounds. After my examination, my only recommendation was that she lose weight. A week later, she was back in my office demanding that I reweigh her.

"Mrs. Beson," I said, "why don't you weigh yourself at home? Every time you come here you are charged for a visit. Why don't you buy yourself a scale and save yourself some money?"

"No," she insisted, "I won't lose weight by myself. If you weigh me, it helps."

So I consented. "You weigh 154 pounds," I told her.

"No," she insisted, "151."

"Check the scale yourself; 154 pounds."

"Only 151," she insisted.

That irritated me! How could an intelligent woman be that stupid? "Look again, can't you read numbers?"

She looked and she explained, "It's only 151. You count my breasts, I don't. They weigh three pounds, so I subtract three from the number on the scale."

"How do you know what your breasts weigh?"

"I weigh them on the kitchen scale."

"Aren't they part of you?"

"No. When I was thirteen, my mother took me to a doctor and I heard him say to her, 'She's got big boobs for a little kid.' Since then, I have never counted my breasts."

Funny, maybe, but that doctor was a heartless fool to say that in front of a child—another example of a member of my profession talking about patients as if they weren't there.

The incident got rid of Hazel Beson's breasts for her, but my thick neck was an issue in my life again.

TREATMENT DAY TWO

I arrive early for my second treatment. I know it's early, but I'm anxious to have it over with. Instead of being sent directly to the treatment room, I am sent to the waiting area. There are two other patients sitting there, and I am confronted by the fact that all three of us have cancer. I have now joined the brotherhood. At least on the surface, none of us seems to be particularly disturbed.

By 9:20 my name has not been called. I tighten up. Why haven't they called me? Did they find something in the CAT scan? The doctor said that they wouldn't treat me with radiation if the CAT scan was positive. I didn't have the courage yesterday to ask for the report. By 9:25 I am in a stew. At 9:30, my appointed time, the technician calls my name. I follow her from the reception room and into the hall. She says nothing, and I ask no questions. I follow her, anxiously waiting to see where we will go. Will she lead me to the doctor's consultation room or into the treatment room? She escorts me into the treatment room. I get onto the table with delight. The treatment is painless and over in ten minutes, and I drive home feeling relieved. My CAT scan must have been negative or they wouldn't have treated me, but I still don't have the courage to ask anyone for a formal report.

Though it was my fault for coming too early, I learned today that one of the cruelest things a doctor can do is to keep a patient waiting. As the sages say, wisdom comes too late.

A few years ago, Barry Leed asked if I would see a patient of his who suffered from arthritis. The patient himself had called for an appointment but had been told it would be two months before I could see him. Dr. Leed suggested that because the patient, John Diamond, was a friend of his and prominent in the community, it would be a favor if I could see him sooner. I looked at my appointment book. I was already overscheduled, but I gave Mr. Diamond an appointment the next morning, before my actual office hours began.

The following morning I started out early in order to see Mr. Diamond, but I was delayed at the hospital. By the time I got to the office, I was a half hour late. The patient was gone. The receptionist reported that he had waited fifteen minutes after his appointment time and then walked out. Soon Dr. Leed was on the phone. Mr. Diamond had complained to him about waiting, but I was forgiven. Would I see the patient tomorrow?

"No," I said, "we would never get along."

I was annoyed then, but today I understand Mr. Diamond's frustration. How in the world did we expect him to wait two months for an appointment? That was cruel. And then, after getting him to my office exceptionally early in the morning, I wasn't there to see him. He was also a busy man with a schedule to keep. Imagine the hostility patients who are kept waiting must feel when they finally make it into the doctor's office. Imagine, I'd never given it any thought before.

TREATMENT DAY THREE

I come early again. I can't seem to help that. I am conducted to my room, which I now understand is not conventional Xray but something called a linear accelerator. The treatment goes rapidly and smoothly. It's over in ten minutes. I get off the table and cheerily say to the technician, "I'll see you tomorrow."

"No, Monday," she corrects me. "We don't treat on weekends."

What? Is this possible? In three days, with three minutes of treatment, they can't have touched many of the cancer cells. At any moment the cells can break loose and flow to other organs. Once the other organs are seeded, it's too late. Why the delay? Why can't they treat on Saturday and Sunday? It's a disgrace. But I offer no comment. I'm not going to challenge the system, at least not now, when I'm totally dependent on it. There's no chance they'd open the office just for me, so there's no point in antagonizing them. I know myself how irritated I get with patients who ask for special privileges. And with X-ray therapy, absolute accuracy is essential. You don't want to ruffle people's feelings or interfere with the routine.

SATURDAY

To me, this is an inauspicious way to begin therapy. I come from a school that believes that once you have joined in combat with cancer, you don't rest. There are no vacations. It's like having a tiger by the tail; you can't let go because only one of you can survive.

I know that therapy is changing, but I am slow to change. Today, breast cancer is first treated by discussion, a biopsy is performed, and then the patient goes home and returns a few days later to discuss her options. More and more patients have only the breast lump removed and then, often, radiation therapy. That's not the way I was brought up. I was taught that once the surgeon put his knife into the cancer cells, pathways were opened for the malignant cells to escape and seed the body. In my day, once the diagnosis was made, there was no delay; there was no awakening the patient for further discussion. The surgeon proceeded with a radical mastectomy. I know that is not the way it is done today, and I understand all the reasons, but so far I am not convinced that the new way is better. I read the favorable statistics, but I remain uneasy.

Once a diagnosis of cancer is made, I don't believe in retreating or stopping. So it is with my X-ray treatment. No one knows for certain which is the better way, whether it is better to treat every day or to have rest periods on weekends. If I had my way, I would treat every day.

I attended a medical meeting where a paper was presented on radiation therapy for cancer. In the program, the title of the paper was given as "Two, One, Two, Two." It sounded like a dance step. When he presented the paper, the radiotherapist explained that he recommended two days of X-ray therapy followed by one day of rest, then two days of X-ray therapy followed by two days of rest, and then a repetition of the cycle, two days of therapy, one day of rest.

Over cocktails that evening I asked him how they had arrived at their formula.

"Very simple," he said. "We work Mondays and Tuesdays, Wednesday is our off day. Thursdays and Fridays are workdays, and Saturdays and Sundays we're off. The program fits our work schedule." I suspect that that's the way they determined my treatment program.

I am used to commanding, but now I have no power. Medical training demands years of subservience. In my case, there were fourteen years: four in medical school, five in residencies, five in the army. Fourteen years of someone else looking over your shoulder. Fourteen years of "Yes sir, no sir, you're right, sir." Then suddenly you're through training and you are on your own. You alone must make decisions that mean life or death, and at first that's scary. Then you taste the power and the glory of being supreme, and you like it. Soon you brook no dissent.

I am the chief. I was chief of medicine in the army. I was chief of medicine in my hospital. I was chief of the arthritis clinic at the medical school. Now they have stripped me of my command. No one asks me what to do. Instead they tell me what to do, and I must submit.

TREATMENT DAY FOUR

This is the start of a new week. Finally I will get five treatments in a row. I have learned not to come too early for my appointment so that I can avoid going into the reception room and being reminded by the other patients' presence that I have a cancer. If I come just on time, I can go directly to the treatment room. But today there is a hitch. The technician directs me to the reception room, and I have to wait ten minutes before someone calls my name. I follow the woman into the hallway, but instead of leading me to my treatment room, she takes me down the hall. I become more and more apprehensive.

"Where are we going?" I demand.

The technician stops, looks at me curiously and says, "Oh, didn't you know? Monday is weigh-in day. We have to weigh you."

I know why. This therapy can cause difficulty in swallowing, loss of appetite, and weight loss; therefore, weight is monitored and the patient is encouraged to eat. He may not be able to eat down the road.

It's the way doctors treated patients fifty years ago. In those days before antibiotics, many an infant died of an infectious disease. When an infant developed an infection accompanied by vomiting and diarrhea, a fat baby with food reserves did better than a thin baby. Like infectious diseases fifty years ago, the course and treatment of cancer today is unpredictable. There may come a time when I can't eat, either because of the spread of the cancer or as a side effect of the therapy. Hence the admonition "Eat while you can. Don't lose weight."

All my life I have been a foodaholic. During the past few years I have controlled the habit, but now all I need is permission to sin again. It's a lot like advising an alcoholic to take a drink.

I knew that I should eat enough to hold my weight or even to gain a few pounds, but no one has advised me what to eat. That's because they don't know what to tell me. The lay literature is full of information, much of it contradictory, and the medical literature is no better. Even worse, the doctors' advice keeps changing. Physicians once told diabetics to eat a diet high in fat because they had no insulin to handle carbohydrates. A typical breakfast tray for diabetics in 1938 included three eggs, three strips of bacon, six pats of butter, no sugar, and very little bread. By 1940 the profession had changed its mind. The diabetic was given plenty of carbohydrates, which were then covered with extra insulin. Today's diabetic diet has changed again to resemble the current normal diet: low in cholesterol and high in complex carbohydrates but not simple sugars.

Diverticulitis is a common bowel condition in which small pockets in the colon become infected. Until recently, the best doctors insisted that patients with diverticulitis eat a diet low in roughage. Today, the same doctors' advice is directly the opposite: "Stuff yourself with roughage."

Patients have often reported to me that a specific diet, or excess vitamins, or macrobiotics, or no starch, or cranberry juice, or you-name-it, had alleviated their illness. I never passed on this advice to other patients because experience had taught me that the diet wouldn't work for the next person. However, I seldom suggested that a patient change his or her program. Over the years I found it was as useless to argue about diet as it was to argue about religion. There is something sacred about a person's dietary ideas; note how many religions have dietary restrictions.

When it comes to weight reduction diets, the problem is worse. Often patients ask, "Is this diet book any good?" My stock answer is, "I know it's very good for the author, but I don't know how good it is for you." Thus far, I've convinced no one, not even my own wife, who was a dietitian.

Fish oil added to the diet is a current fad, but it's not new. Fifty years ago tons of horrible-tasting cod liver oil were pushed down kids' gullets. Cod liver oil is rich in vitamin D, so we concentrated the vitamin D in capsules and gave magnum doses of it to our arthritic patients. We continued that for a few years until some of the subjects died of calcium deposits in the kidneys caused by the vitamin D.

There are some dietary admonitions that seem sound: low salt for hypertension, low cholesterol for cardiac patients. But I wondered how seriously the medical profession takes dietary information after my mother-in-law's recent hospital experience. I was impressed with the ease with which her physicians implanted a cardiac pacemaker in her. A few years ago, this would have been a major surgical event. Now it was a minor procedure. The cardiac floor was particularly impressive. The nursing station was straight out of *Star Trek*: banks of television monitors, flashing electrocardiograms, and ringing bells, all supervised by efficient angels in stiff white starched uniforms. Super efficient, super scientific.

The system broke down with Rose's first morning's breakfast of steak and hash brown potatoes. It was a pure cholesterol meal. When I questioned the nurse, she said it was an error. An error? With all the computers and all the scientific stuff, the same error repeated that has bugged hospitals from their very beginning. I asked to see the next day's menu. I was advised that patients could choose for themselves. I looked at the selections. For those who wanted it and who were religious in following the low-cholesterol diet advised for cardiac patients, there were fruit, dry toast, and coffee. For those who wanted to live it up, there were scrambled eggs, bacon, and hash browns—all this on a cardiac floor.

My grandparents never heard of cholesterol. When they settled in Omaha at the turn of the century, both sets of grandparents lived side by side. In those days, garages were separate from the house. But who had a car? One set of grandparents, the Mittlemans, converted their garage into a barn in which they kept a horse and two cows. The other set, the Rosenbaums, converted their garage into a henhouse. Our family income was meager, but food was plentiful. From the cows we had fresh milk, thick butter, rich sweet and sour cream, and cheese. The hens furnished daily eggs. This diet was supplemented with beef at least three days a week, chicken, fish on Fridays, and whole grain breads. Fruit and vegetables were available only in season, a short season in Nebraska. To this diet my family added copious amounts of chicken fat. There were no additional vitamins or food supplements. One grandfather died at the age of sixty-eight, the other at eighty-four. Both grandmothers lived into their mid-nineties. None of their children raised in America died prematurely; some are still living in their eighties and nineties. Each generation was an inch or two taller and sturdier. They never knew of nutritionists, so they never knew that their diet was all wrong.

What do I believe about all this dietary confusion? I am convinced that there is no simple best diet for everyone. There are too many genetic differences between people. Some can handle fats, some can't; some thrive on milk, some don't; and some can handle candy, though a diabetic can't.

The statistics we have today seem to show that the lean do better than the fat, that a low-cholesterol, high-roughage diet makes sense. That's my opinion at this writing, but to generalize on diet is like giving the same pill to all people for all illnesses. And I've seen the statistics change a few times in my time.

TREATMENT DAY FIVE

This day everything goes well. There's no wait in the reception area, and the treatment is bang, bang, over in ten minutes. I get off the hard table, button my shirt, and am happily prepared to leave when the technician sternly says, "Wait a minute. Don't you know it's Tuesday?"

"What's special about Tuesday?"

"Doctor's day," she answers, as if I were mentally incompetent. "You must see the doctor every Tuesday. Don't be in a hurry, I'll find a room where you can wait for him."

She disappears and comes back in five minutes with the news, "All the rooms are full. The doctor is too busy today. He'll see you next week."

That's when my mood changes. I was just getting used to the routine, and suddenly there is no routine. Five minutes ago I was told that Tuesday was the most important day of the week, and then suddenly I am told that it's unimportant. Wait another week, the doctor is too busy.

I have some very important questions to ask. Specifically, what was the result of my CAT scan? I have been told that I would not be treated if the CAT scan showed that the lymph nodes were involved. Up until now, because I have had four treatments, I have assumed that there were no enlarged nodes, but I know better. I know of cases where medical reports were filed in the chart by a secretary and never reviewed by the doctor. This type of error is especially likely to occur in large medical centers where personnel are constantly changing. I have had the experience of taking over the care of a patient from doctors who were changing wards, and on reviewing the patient's record I've seen adverse medical reports that were ignored. There could be only one explanation: they were never read by the doctor. Medical rules dictate that only the attending physician can discuss laboratory or Xray results with the patient. Other personnel are forbidden to reveal what is in the hospital record. It is important that I talk with Dr. Reed to be sure that he has reviewed my CAT scan, or, at the very least, read the reports. I must hear his opinion on the course of my treatment so far. The only time I saw him, he went in and out of the treatment room without giving me the courtesy of a word.

Okay. Here I'm not a big-time specialist, I'm a patient. But doctors should talk to patients.

With that in mind, I gather up my courage, go to the appointment desk, and advise the secretary that no matter how long it takes, I am perfectly willing to wait to see the doctor.

"There is no use waiting," she tells me. "The doctor is too busy today, and he has already left this floor for his rounds at another hospital."

TREATMENT DAY SIX

A s I drive to the hospital for my treatment, I listen to the car radio. First there are news commentaries, then a talk show follows.

The guest is a published author who dislikes doctors, and the radio host greets him with great enthusiasm. The author is a self-anointed, self-appointed authority on cancer. He says that doctors advised him that he had hopeless cancer, so he cured himself. He studied Indian lore and found a desert plant from which he brewed tea. He drank the tea, cleansed his blood and his soul, and thus eradicated the cancer. Now he is ready to share his secret with the rest of the world. His book, which sells for only fifteen dollars, tells it all in a more detailed way, but if you possibly can, come to his lecture tonight. He would like to make it free so that all mankind could benefit from his work. He is not selfish like doctors, but he does need to meet expenses, so admission is a mere three dollars. If you elect to buy the book, he only makes a dollar.

The host is enthusiastic.

"Why do doctors oppose you?" he asks.

And the expert replies, "The answer is obvious. Think what a doctor charges for each visit. Opposition to me is a conspiracy. The doctors are protecting their income."

I get angry at the guy, but in my present state of mind I can understand his appeal. At this point, my own doctor is grim. He promises nothing. Here's someone who says he has a cheap, painless cure. A charlatan for sure, but no wonder people follow him.

TREATMENT DAY SEVEN

Except for my voice, I feel fine. For the first time since the start of my illness some close friends come over for the evening. A few of them greet me with sad looks on their faces. I understand. How do you greet a friend who is dying of cancer?

When the friends leave, the woman particularly are solicitous. Now they kiss me full on the lips. They linger a little longer and some of them rub my back.

I think this is great, but it's ten years too late. Why did those women wait so long to give me a good kiss? They're hard to understand. And then I laugh, remembering a patient. Dick Lang had asked me to see her in consultation in the hospital. First I knocked on her room door, respecting her privacy. Even in the hospital I've never barged into a room unannounced. I waited, and when a soft voice bade me to come in, I entered. The room was dimly lit, and there was the patient, sitting on her bed, stark naked and smiling. I knew from her chart that she was forty-five, but she had the body of a sixteen-year-old. Her long black hair hung to her shoulders, and heavy lashes emphasized her dark eyes.

Before I could gather my composure, she asked quickly, "Who are you?"

"I'm Dr. Rosenbaum. Dr. Lang asked me to see you in consultation."

"Oh, pardon me," she said. And with that she got off

her bed, walked to the closet, put on a robe, returned again to sit sedately on her bed, and quite calmly said, "I'm ready now, doctor."

For whom, I wondered? But I never found out. It's one of the never-solved mysteries of my long medical career.

TREATMENT DAY EIGHT

FRIDAY THE RABBI CAME

D ee breaks it to me gently. "Rabbi Kohn called this morning."

"What did he want?"

"He's coming to see you."

I am irritated. "Why? I'm not a regular synagogue-goer. He has never called on me before. I don't need condolences, and I don't want sympathy."

"I couldn't say no," Dee explains.

"I would have had no trouble," I retort. "One thing that happens after you're faced with death is that you tell people what you think. Old people aren't eccentric. They've just lost their inhibitions. When's he coming?"

"Today."

Later in the day, through the window, I watch his approach. I have to admire him. He is doing something I have never been able to do: call on a cancer patient at home. It's all I can do to visit a terminal patient in the hospital room. What can a doctor say to a patient when therapy fails? I always try to refer the cancer patient. Let the consultant explain our failures. I can't handle my own grief for the patient enough to be much help—or so I've always thought.

I meet the rabbi at the door, escort him to the library,

and challenge him as soon as he takes a seat: "Did you come to pray with me?"

"No, I've learned better. When I first entered the rabbinate, I used to make hospital rounds with a little black prayer book in my hands, until I realized that it looked to my patients like I was going to give them the last rites."

"You mean Jews don't believe in prayer?"

"Quite the contrary," he assures me, "but they're accustomed to individual prayer with God. They don't need intermediaries like a young, presumptuous rabbi."

"Have patients received you more cordially without the prayer book?"

"Not really. Once, when I was making hospital calls, I went into a room, and before I could stop him the patient began to recite all his symptoms. When he finished he demanded, 'Doctor, what can you do for me?'

" 'We can pray,' I answered.

" 'Pray, hell, man! I'm sick, do something!' "

"Sounds practical to me," I say to the rabbi.

"Religion can be practical too," he answers. "I'll give you an example. A Mormon friend of mine had a young widowed daughter. In their religion, marriages are made in heaven for eternity. Therefore, a widow can remarry only a widower. Otherwise, when they get to heaven to reunite with their first mates, one party would be left without a mate. So what happens? She falls madly in love with a never-married man. He reciprocates her love, but marriage is impossible. So they confront the elders of the congregation with the problem. Do you know how they solved it?"

"No," I answer.

"They got married. The elders suggest that they leave the solution to God when they got to heaven."

"I like that," I tell the rabbi. "Sounds like the way my grandmother would have solved the problem. When I was a little boy I used to take my toys apart. She would warn me, 'Take it apart and you won't be able to put it together again, and it will never run,' and that was her theology. She insisted, 'You have to have faith. If you ask too many questions, if you search too deeply, you might end up with nothing.' "

"Have you ever had a patient recover from cancer when you didn't expect it?" the rabbi asks.

"Do Jews believe in miracles?" I reply.

"Well, Moses split the Red Sea and brought water from a rock."

"You're a master at evasion," I tell him. "But there are some cases that I've never forgotten, like Angelo Costello—after all these years, I can still remember his name. I was a hospital resident, and in reviewing his previous records I learned that five years before I saw him, Angelo had been advised that his wife was dying of cancer. I hated to revive old memories, but I had to ask the question: 'What happened to your wife?'

"He laughed. 'She's great! She's alive. The doctors scared the hell out of me. When I took her home to die, I had to tell her what the doctors said and all she said was, "They're wrong. God has told me they are wrong." Instead of getting worse, she got better, and she's still okay.' "

"How do you account for that?" asks the rabbi.

"Easy. Wrong diagnosis. Every doctor has had similar cases. If the patient survives and the records are reviewed, there usually was a mistake. Either an X ray was misread or a pathological slide was misinterpreted. That usually accounts for the so-called 'faith cures.' There are cases where even after an autopsy, the cause of death cannot be determined. I've known good pathologists to disagree on whether a biopsy is benign or malignant. Can you imagine what a hell that is for the patient? If you aren't treated, you may die of cancer; if you are treated, you may die from needless therapy."

"Have you ever known of serious cases, accurately diagnosed, where people still recovered without medical treatment?" the rabbi persists.

"Yes," I tell him. "I had one case where I was certain that the patient had a cancer, yet she recovered without medical treatment. I can't tell you why."

The rabbi rose to go.

"What's your hurry?" I ask.

"It's Friday," he explains. "I have to be home before sundown to prepare for the Sabbath."

"I thought so. You're copping out. You're no better than I am. You timed your visit so that you could get away after only a few minutes with the sick guy."

And then we both grin. It was clear that the rabbi's medicine had made me feel better.

SATURDAY

It's a day of rest. No treatment. Joyce, an old friend whom I haven't seen in years, calls. She has heard the terrible news, and she and her husband want to come and visit us. I urge her to come over, but she never shows up.

I've never thought about it before, but having a serious illness, or serious pain like many of my own patients do, is an isolating experience. Other people's troubles may be hard to relate to: my neighbor's preoccupation with remodeling his terrace is hard for me to get worked up about. And some of my friends have trouble dealing with me. My cancer becomes like a litmus test: who will be able to face it with me, who will not? I understand Joyce. It's hard to visit a dying cancer patient. I understand, but I'm hurt.

TREATMENT DAY NINE

The Xray treatment in the morning was uneventful. That evening Dr. Cade, the doctor who did the first biopsy and missed the diagnosis, calls.

I don't want to talk to him. I excuse myself by saying that my throat is too sore to talk, and I pass the phone to my wife. She is in tears as she listens to his explanations: he was reassured by the negative biopsy; he's sorry; what can he do?

What can he do? The die has been cast; the delay may have been fatal. I won't know that for a long time.

I wonder if he's calling because he is truly sorry or if he is trying to forestall a malpractice suit. I have already been advised to sue for malpractice. As a doctor, I understand his feelings; I, too, have missed diagnoses. Every error is followed by a period of depression and remorse and anxiety. But that does not compare to the anguish of the patient and the family.

There is no such thing as an infallible doctor. We have all made mistakes. I knew of a physician who insisted he had never made a wrong diagnosis. He was dangerous because in refusing to recognize his errors, he never learned. He conveniently forgot about Mrs. Dunkler, a woman in her fifties who had consulted him. If there ever was a neurotic, she was it, a champion chronic complainer. Every week there was a new symptom to investigate. When she began to complain of indigestion, her symptoms were so persistent that the infallible doctor had her examined by other specialists. After three normal stomach X rays by three different radiologists, she died within a year of the onset of her indigestion. The autopsy revealed cancer of the stomach. Today, with modern flexible gastroscopes, the doctor could have made the correct diagnosis.

Dr. Cade's sin was not in missing a diagnosis. His error was that he had not kept up and had not used the most modern, advanced techniques.

Because I am a colleague, I cannot entertain the thought of a malpractice suit against him. I understand how doctors feel about the threat of malpractice. It is an affront to them because they have dedicated their lives to doing good and the very word malpractice means doing evil. A malpractice suit produces a scar that lasts for life, but there has to be a way to hold physicians accountable. And many patients suffer more than a scar from inadequate diagnosis or treatment. I'm not going to sue Dr. Cade, though other people, with justification, might.

We have been colleagues and acquaintances for a long time, but I am afraid that our friendship is over.

TREATMENT DAY TEN

Today is Tuesday, doctor's day. This will be the first time I have seen the doctor since my initial visit. I'm anxious, yet relieved that the visit is short and perfunctory.

"How do you feel?" he asks.

"Okay."

"No sore throat?"

"No."

"No cough?"

"No."

"No trouble swallowing?"

"No."

"Skin sore?"

"No."

I'm afraid to say yes to anything for fear that he might stop therapy. "What's going to happen?" I ask.

And he says shortly, "You're going to feel worse."

That's not the way I treat patients; I always try to reassure them. I think that's an important factor in helping them get well. But these cancer therapists are a different breed; they are absolutely honest.

After I leave, I realize I did not ask, "What did my CAT scan show? Were my lymph nodes involved?" I still do not want to know, I guess. I have always been critical of patients who spend their office visit in idle chatter and then, as they start to leave, say, "Oh, I forgot to mention that there is a lump in my breast." Now I'm acting just like them. As I gained experience in my practice, I learned to end the patient interview with the question, "Do you have any questions or anything else you want to discuss?" More and more doctors are learning to use that technique. But apparently not mine.

TREATMENT DAY ELEVEN

Now I wonder if I should have gotten a second opinion regarding the X-ray therapy. Nothing seems to be happening, and I am discouraged. My voice is still raspy, and I don't seem to be experiencing any side effects from the X-ray treatment. My throat isn't sore, and I have no trouble swallowing. This makes me wonder if it's doing anything at all.

Every three months the technicians change. They rotate to avoid staleness and to learn how to operate the new machines. To me that's nonsense. Hitting the target exactly is the important thing. I resent having anyone learn on me.

But it turns out I am delighted by this change. Debbie, the new technician, is a joy. My neck must be exposed for treatment. She doesn't wait for me to unbutton my collar; she unbuttons it for me and neatly tucks it in.

When the treatment is over, the lights go on and the table is lowered. She holds both my hands to help me off the table. She meets my gaze full on. She straightens my collar and buttons my shirt. It's okay with me. For almost the first time, I feel that someone's taking care of me and cares what happens to me.

I wonder if my wife would mind. When my father was past ninety, he became too much of a burden for my mother, and we prevailed upon her to hire day help. The first week my mother was delighted. The second week she fired the girl, explaining, "All the girl does is sit by his side. They hold hands, she kisses him, he kisses her. I think he likes her better than he likes me. I don't have to pay her eight dollars an hour for that."

TREATMENT DAY TWELVE

When I arrive in the waiting room, a little boy of about four is there. His head is shaved clean, and the treatment sites are tattooed on his bare scalp. He laughs as he plays with a toy truck. A man of about fifty, holding a hospital chart, is reading a book. My guess is that he has leukemia. A woman's head is covered with a scarf. That means that she has lost her hair, probably from receiving both X-ray therapy and chemotherapy. We all wait our turns patiently and silently until an old lady comes in. I know from her peach-colored apron and the pin-on plastic nameplate that she is a volunteer, come to cheer us up. When she offers us magazines and hard candy, we all refuse, even the little boy. We remain silent as she chatters away, offering us words of consolation. It is as if we are united in a conspiracy of pride. We know how serious our problems are and what our chances are. We're rejecting the ''easy fix'' the old lady is offering. Poor thing. She doesn't have cancer, but she is old and probably depressed and lonely. Maybe her only relief is volunteering to work with those she feels are worse off—us, the cancer patients.

We are all receiving therapy, so we all must be hopeful. But we now know that we are not immortal. Until recently I attributed my illnesses to colds, flu, or dietary indiscretions, all self-limiting and curable. Now I recognize that I am mortal, and every symptom that I have I attribute to cancer. If I cough, I think I have cancer of the lungs. If I ache, I suspect that my cancer has spread to my bones. I don't mention these symptoms to anyone for fear that my doctor will think me foolish or that, in fact, my cancer has spread to my bones.

For the past few days I have been nauseated. I would like to attribute the symptom to the X-ray treatment, but when I do discuss it, the doctors assure me that I am not getting enough X rays to cause nausea. If that's the case, then I am sure that the cancer has spread to my liver.

If symptoms persist, I will have to face it and have a gastrointestinal examination. I hate the thought of it; it's a messy procedure. The stomach X ray isn't too bad, just a swallow of some barium that tastes like chalk. The part

I dread is the laxatives and enemas for the colon examination.

I have a dilemma. If I complain, I will have tests. If I don't complain—no tests, but possibly a missed diagnosis. Unfortunately, unlike the usual patient, I happen to know that tests are not necessarily innocuous. Doctors love to do them; it makes medicine seem more scientific. In recent years, because a missed diagnosis may mean a malpractice suit, physicians have had a tendency to overtest; it's called defensive medicine. The practice is understandable. If a diagnosis is missed and there is a test that would have detected the disease, there is no defense in the courtroom. That is very similar to Dr. Cade failing to use the nasopharyngoscope on me.

Many tests are harmless, but some require injections of a drug to which, on rare occasions, there can be a fatal allergic reaction. Some procedures, such as a needle biopsy of the liver or cardiac catheterization, are known as invasive, where an instrument is introduced into the body. Like any surgical procedure, these tests carry a real, albeit small, risk.

Even tests that are in themselves innocuous may lead to trouble by obscuring a diagnosis. Ten percent of all laboratory tests are in error. I have divided one blood sample into three parts and sent the individual samples to three different laboratories. I got back three different results! In the hands of an inexperienced or careless physician, false results can lead to unnecessary treatment and procedures.

When I was an intern, pneumonia was the leading cause of death. It afflicted infants in the first year of life and adults in the prime of life. One out of four patients died. Because doctors had no treatment, they would argue over such details as to how many aspirin tablets a day to prescribe or whether the windows in the patient's room should be open or closed.

At the hospital I trained in, the chief of staff would appear every morning dressed in a dark suit, a white shirt, and a dull silk tie. He would be followed by residents and interns all in white and medical students in white jackets but ordinary civilian pants. When the large group entered the wards, all nurses stood at attention.

This personage, with all his prestige, could do nothing to cure pneumonia, but he *could* order laboratory tests. At that time we were able to classify thirty-two different types of pneumococcus that could cause the disease. When a pneumonia patient was admitted to the hospital, no matter what time of the day or night, the intern was awakened to test the sputum and determine the type of pneumococcus. The next morning on hospital rounds, I would walk in the wake of this great man, who would turn to the chief resident and say, "What did the sputum show?"

The chief resident would turn to the assistant resident behind him. "What did the sputum show?"

The assistant resident would turn to me, the intern, and ask, "What did the sputum show?"

I would sleepily respond, "Type IV pneumococcus." And the information would be passed up the line from me to the assistant, from the assistant to the resident, from the resident to the doctor, who would knowingly nod his head.

One morning, when I could stand it no longer, I blurted out, "Now that you guys know the pneumococcus type, what are you going to do with the information?"

They all stopped and looked at me in astonishment. I was almost thrown out of the hospital for being so impertinent.

If I continue to complain about my nausea, as I envision the scenario, a gastroenterologist will be asked to see me in consultation. Before he comes, a student will take my history once more. Then he will examine me completely, even checking me for a hernia and doing a rectal examination—for he has to learn. After him, the resident will come. The resident will surely be a young girl. She will ask the same questions, and even some more personal ones, and then do a more thorough exam than the student did, even checking me for a hernia. Though they were done only two weeks ago, she will order a repeat of the blood tests, the urinalysis, the electrocardiogram, the chest X ray, and in addition, stomach and colon X rays. The nurse will give me containers for urine and three little boxes in which to collect my stools on three separate days. Finally, the busy gastroenterologist will appear. If he is thorough, he will repeat the entire history and physical. If he is too busy, he will accept the resident's reports. The stomach and colon X rays will turn out to be normal, but one stool specimen will show a trace of blood. Never mind that the test is so sensitive that if I ate some red meat, or overbrushed my teeth, or took some aspirin tablets, the test would read "Blood." Now, like bloodhounds, the doctors have a clue, and they are on the scent. They will not give up. I will have to have gastroscopic and proctoscopic examinations. I will object to the proctoscopic exam, and they will insist that it's good for me. "Everyone over sixty-five should have a proctoscopic to detect early colon cancer," they'll tell me. I wonder how many of them or other doctors my age have had one voluntarily. Not many, I'm sure.

When these tests are normal, a powwow will be held. First they will ask the student his opinion, and he will say, "He's old but he's not senile. He could have cirrhosis of the liver. He says he doesn't drink, but drinkers never admit it."

The resident will say, "His marital life seems to be okay, so I know he's not functional. His blood pressure was up when I examined him. I once had a patient complain of nausea, and it turned out to be the heart, angina. But he's seventy, so I don't think we should be too aggressive."

The gastroenterologist will say, "They've already made one mistake on him. If he complains, it's probably for real. We can't afford to miss, he's a doctor. Let's talk to him about doing an arteriogram of his heart or a liver scan and a needle biopsy of the liver."

When they discuss it with me, I will say no. I know the risks. Coronary artery X rays are usually safe, but one patient in a thousand ends up with a stroke or dies. A liver biopsy can result in life-threatening bleeding. Besides, if they find something, it is unlikely that they will be able to do anything. I'll be like the pneumonia patient in the 1930s: now that they know, what can they do?

When I say "No," they will tell my wife that I am stubborn, so they can't be held responsible for a missed diagnosis. I've seen the show before, and it's not for me; so I don't complain.

If I had a patient who was acting like I am, I would probably ask him or her to get another doctor. Or rather, I *would have* asked—in the past.

TREATMENT DAY THIRTEEN

The receptionist apologizes for chewing gum.

"It's not very professional," I admonish her.

"I can't help it," she explains. "It's not real chewing gum. I'm trying to quit smoking. It's nicotine gum."

"You? You smoke?" I ask in surprise. "Who better than you can see the end results of smoking?"

"I know," she says, "but I can't quit."

I reflect on how easy it is to believe that it can only happen to others and not to oneself, and how hard it is to give up a present pleasure for a future benefit.

When the first doctor to successfully remove a lung for

lung cancer reported the results to an assembly of physicians, he was loudly applauded. Then he added, "Evidence is rapidly accumulating that smoking is a cause of lung cancer." And with that he calmly lit a big black cigar and placed it in his mouth as he walked off the stage. He subsequently died of lung cancer.

How far should a physician go in seeing to it that the patient complies with his orders? It has been estimated that one third of patients do not follow their doctor's advice. A colleague of mine, Jay Blatt, would not tolerate such disobedience. If he encountered one of his patients smoking, he would pull the cigarette from the offender's mouth and snuff it out. In a restaurant, if he saw a patient of his eating forbidden food, he would publicly berate the poor soul and demand that the waitress remove the offending dishes.

When some people get sick, they *want* the physician to take control. Even if they're very competent in their lives, they want to turn the responsibility for their illness over to someone else. One of my patients was like that. She accused me of being a chauvinist, and when I asked her why she didn't change doctors, she said, "I like being directed by a strong man."

I don't follow my patients into restaurants to see what they're eating, but I think I do treat them as if *I'm* the boss. That's true of both men *and* women. That patient was wrong to call me a chauvinist. I think I must have been one of the earliest women's libbers.

SATURDAY

This weekend, we babysit our eldest grandchildren, ten-year-old Steve and seven-year-old Laura. Often we play cards with them, simple games like hearts, old maid, maybe even five-card poker. But today we have a surprise. To cheer me up, their parents have secretly been teaching them bridge. When they demonstrate their new skill to us, Dee and I are sure that they are the smartest, brightest children in the world.

Often, after we have played our games, I tell the children stories. My grandfather used to tell me about the czar, the cossacks, the pogroms. My father told my children about crossing the ocean in steerage, in the bowels of the ship, and subsisting only on coarse black bread. I tell these children about my boyhood in Omaha, about snow and below-zero weather, and how, in that weather, I would walk a mile to school, four times a day, because we had to go home for lunch. They don't understand my stories. Living in Portland, they have never experienced below-zero weather, and they cannot conceive of a family without a car. Today, because I have no voice to tell stories, we decide to spend the evening going out for dinner, and we all agree on Chinese food.

Portland is saturated with Chinese restaurants. Besides those in Chinatown, there is one in every neighborhood, sometimes two to a block. In the old days, the choice was simple; there was only one kind of Chinese food, Cantonese. For ten dollars I could stuff my family of six with egg roll, won ton soup, fried rice, chow mein, fried shrimp, and fortune cookies. Because of my relationship to the Chinese community, the restaurant's proprietor would often refuse to give me a bill. I would insist on paying, and then the boys would be sent home with huge sacks of fortune cookies and candy bars.

Nowadays, with the influx of immigrants from Taiwan, Hong Kong, and Shanghai, Chines restaurants offer regional cuisines: Cantonese, Mandarin, Szechuan, Taiwan, Hunan. As often happens, Dee and I want Cantonese, Steve wants Mandarin, and Laura demands pot stickers. So we compromise on Japanese food, but both children insist that there has to be a sushi bar.

"Such sophisticated palates," I tell Dee. "I would never have eaten raw fish at their age."

"What about herring when you were a child?" Dee asks.

"What about it? When I was a kid, everyone I knew ate herring, boiled potatoes, and black bread." Then I laugh, realizing that herring is raw fish. "You know," I continue, "we never see ourselves as we really are. My doctors irritate me. They keep me waiting, and after I wait an hour, they only spend five minutes with me. I get irritated but I don't complain. Do you know why? Because I've been doing the same thing to my patients for fifty years."

TREATMENT DAY FOURTEEN

Today I have a new concern: the skin of my neck is turning pink. Radiation therapy can cause serious skin burns. I ask the technician if some patients develop enough skin irritation to necessitate stopping treatment. She smiles and says, "Yes" but doesn't bother to examine my skin, and I don't insist.

I am afraid to tell her about my skin. I don't want my treatment interrupted. I should ask to see Dr. Reed and leave the decision to him as to whether or not to continue treatment, but I can't bring myself to do that. Every day of my life as a doctor, I have had to make decisions that could mean life or death for someone else. I always did my best, but I am human. At times there would be alternative pathways that I didn't know about. On rare occasions, I have strayed and taken the wrong road, and both I and the patient have had to live with the decision. At first I would so agonize over each decision that I seriously considered changing professions, but as time went on, the process became more automatic and was based on statistical probabilities. I adjusted. "It's the life of a doctor," I told myself.

But now I am the patient. I don't want any mistakes, and I don't want to depend on statistics. I know that doctors are human, and though Dr. Reed has had more experience than I have had with problems like this, I can't let go of command and let him make the decision.

So I do a dumb thing. I say nothing and permit the treatment to go on. Because the redness is so mild and can't be seen unless it's particularly looked for, no one except me is aware of it. It is stupid. I could get a serious skin burn that will trouble me for the rest of my life.

TREATMENT DAY FIFTEEN

Today is Tuesday, doctor's day. The only thing that gives me any security is that I am in a routine. Doing exactly the same thing every day hypnotizes me. I focus on the routine instead of on my problem.

But today, there is a change. On the first day, as a patient at the medical school, I was given a plastic card, like a credit card, with my name and number on it. It is my ticket of admission. I have to present it to the receptionist at every visit for imprinting on a sheet of paper that goes into my chart and to another sheet that goes to the business office for billing. It is an impersonal system, but how else can it be done? The medical school probably has over a million charts on file; I know, because in our small office we already have accumulated sixty thousand charts. When I present my card to the receptionist, she smiles and says, "We're changing computer systems. After you leave here, you will have to go to the record room for a new card and a new number."

It may seem like a small thing, but it upsets me. With a million records, it's not hard to lose one. I have known it to happen, and sometimes the chart is never found. Then everyone has to work by guess and by memory, and it is hard to reconstruct a history when a number of people have seen the patient. Besides, to get a new number, I have to go to another building. That means at least another lost hour that morning.

I vent my hostility on the poor receptionist. "Why can't it all be done by mail? The record room is in another building, and it means a walk across the campus, more elevators and another wait.''

"I don't know. I just work here,'' she tells me.

After my treatment is over, the technician helps me off the table, escorts me to a small cubicle, and places my chart in a box beside the door.

I anxiously await the doctor's visit, hoping he'll offer me some assurance. He enters, nods, and gives me a weak smile. I watch his face carefully as he palpates my neck, trying to read his opinion of what he feels. Imagine me, a physician, reduced to such a state. Why don't I just ask him what he feels? Then he looks into my throat with a tongue blade and brings out his mirror. I don't say a word while he sticks the mirror into my throat to look into my larynx. Then I can see the look of frustration on his face as he puts his mirror aside and says, ''Oh, I forgot. We can't visualize your vocal cords with the mirror.'' Why can't he remember that he tried to look at my cords with the mirror once before and wasn't successful?

I know that he has not been trained to use the new fiberoptic nasopharyngoscope. I am frustrated and worried because I would like to know if anything is happening, but I don't want to insult him by suggesting that he call the resident for help.

''How do you feel?'' he asks.

''I feel great. I don't feel any different than when I started.'' He can't see my neck because my collar is buttoned. He doesn't ask about my skin, and I don't tell him.

''It's too early,'' he tells me. ''You're going to get hoarser and your throat is going to get sorer.''

That doesn't make me feel any better, but I gather enough courage to ask, ''What are my odds?''

''About an eighty-five percent cure rate,'' he says, for the ninth or tenth time.

''I hope you're right.'' My mind doesn't focus on the 85 percent cure rate, it concentrates on the 15 percent failure rate. So I continue, "I always thought that X rays are carcinogenic and could cause cancer."

"True, they used to, when we overtreated," he blandly replies, "but with modern X rays and modern methods, we can destroy cancer cells and leave the healthy cells intact." He then gives me another smile, stands up, obviously reluctant to discuss the matter any further, and walks out. I don't stop him. I know Tuesday is a busy day for him, and I know how he feels. There are days when the doctor has had it. He just can't talk to patients anymore.

As I walk slowly to the record room, I try to understand what's happening to me. They tell me that I am being treated by X ray. X means unknown. I can't see, hear, taste, feel, or smell the X rays. I have no way of knowing if anything is happening or if the machine is working. The skin burn doesn't necessarily mean the cancer is being touched. The radiologist assures me that something will happen and asks me to have faith. Is he a priest?

I suppose I have no choice but to have faith, but I can't really manage it because I myself have sometimes prescribed X rays knowing that, at best, they would be palliative. I have never said to a patient, "Let's quit." If one treatment failed, I would shift to another, even though I knew it was hopeless. That's the way I was taught. Don't tell the patient, always keep trying. I know that nowadays, the emphasis is on being truthful, on sharing all the facts with the patient, no matter how gruesome they are. But there are exceptions. There is supposed to be professional courtesy; doctors don't treat a colleague like a patient. It is possible that I am being spared the truth.

I still do not know what to say to a doomed patient. A visit to a terminal patient is very painful to me. As I approach the room, my muscles tighten and I feel anxious. I know that the patient will watch every movement and every expression. Since my presence in the room seems to give the patient comfort, I tarry a little longer than usual, but really I can't wait to get out. I am relieved when I walk into the hallway. As I close the door, I am already preparing myself for tomorrow's visit. As the end approaches, each visit will become more painful.

At the end of her days, when my mother lay dying in a hospital, it was terribly hard for me to visit her. I knew from her eyes and her mannerisms that she wanted to know what was happening, but I couldn't tell her that she was dying. She was not assured by the important medical consultants and the innumerable tests. All of us knew what was happening, but no one could utter the words. On the day of her death she told me that her greatest comfort was from her night nurse, a Catholic sister who during her late rounds would spend a few minutes with her to visit and tell her, "I am praying for you."

"Imagine," she told me, "a Catholic sister praying for a Jewish woman." She held my hands and looked at me but said nothing. I knew from her look what she was saying: Will you pray for me? Will you say Kaddish, the prayer for the dead, according to our tradition?

I did not answer, because to say anything would be to acknowledge impending death. As a professional, I knew that the end was near, but as a son, I could not emotionally accept that. I have never in all my life been able to say to a patient, "You are going to die." That is the way we talk to a condemned murderer. Why do that to the innocent patient? Hope is essential. To rob a patient of hope is cruel. Once in a while, the doctor is wrong and a miracle occurs.

Everyone agrees that a cancer patient must be told, but how much should he or she be told? I have known doctors to advocate disciplining colleagues who offered too optimistic a prognosis to cancer patients. The rule today is "Tell it like it is."

At staff conferences I have heard young doctors, nurses, and social workers describe how stoic patients were when they were told they had cancer. One hears such phrases as "He took it like a man" or "She did not even shed a tear." My own reaction is that what the young doctor is seeing is shock and disbelief, misinterpreted as calmness and acceptance of one's fate.

I once heard a doctor say to a patient, "Go home. The treatment has failed. We have nothing more to offer you."

"Do you mean go home to die?" the patient asked.

"Don't we all die eventually?" the doctor responded.

That doctor represents a modern school of thought. When I graduated from medical school, no physician would say to a patient, "You have cancer." The family would be told but the patient, never. As therapy improved and patients became more informed, the rules shifted to, "Tell the truth directly and bluntly." Time proved that to be a cruel and unusual punishment. Now we teach medical students, "Listen to patients; they'll tell you how much and what they want to know; tell them only what they can handle."

The dictum sounds so sensible, so simple, but is it? Before Katherine Buerger went to surgery, she said to me, "When I wake up, tell me the truth. If it's cancer, I need to know. My husband has had a stroke, and I am our sole support. Don't hide anything from me."

I repeated her instructions to Dr. Shwartz, the surgeon. After her operation, he told her bluntly and directly, "You have inoperable, untreatable lung cancer."

When I visited Katie the next morning, in spite of her pain she was bright and cheerful. She told me, "Dr. Shwartz is wonderful, so honest and direct. I love him."

When I visited her the second morning, she asked, "How good is Dr. Shwartz? What are his credentials?"

The third morning, she said to me, "I don't want Dr. Shwartz to come and see me anymore. I can't stand him. Please, take care of me and keep him away."

It was not Dr. Shwartz's fault. It takes a very sensitive, astute, experienced physician to know what to say to the dying patient. There aren't too many such doctors.

So, which treatment am I getting? The old-fashioned

one, "Keep up their hopes," or the modern one, "Tell it like it is"?

My doctors are in the older age group. I'm going to stick with them. I'm not going to let any of their young residents or students get near me.

I finally arrive at the record room, where I have to wait a half hour while my card is being changed. When they give me my new card, I look at it and find that my name is spelled right but they have left off my title, M.D. They have completely reduced me to the status of a patient.

TREATMENT DAY SIXTEEN

I awake with a foul taste in my mouth. When I was a child, doctors made a great to-do about checking the pulse and inspecting the tongue. If the tongue was coated, the prescription was a laxative. I look at my tongue in the mirror. It looks normal. Is the foul taste due to the dying cancer cells or the dying good cells?

August is a bad month to receive therapy. Too many vacations. The technicians come and go.

Today it's Ted. I have confidence in him. I have seen him around the department since day one, and I think he must be the head technician because of the way he orders the others around.

Today I feel secure about the treatment. Ted quickly and efficiently centers the tube on my tattoo marks. The cassettes click into place with a reassuring snap, the lights go on, he scurries out of the room to safety, the lights go off. The whirring sound begins. I know that I am to receive one minute of X ray, thirty seconds on each side. I always count the seconds, it helps relieve the strain. I start the count: one, two, then click, the lights go on, red lights flash. Something has happened to interrupt the treatment. The technician runs into the room and attempts to reassure me. "The emergency switch went off, shutting off the machine. Don't worry. You didn't get any overexposure."

"What set off the emergency?" I asked.

"You're on the linear accelerator. That's man-made X ray. It depends on a vacuum tube. When the tube starts to age, it is prone to go out. This one is toward the end of its life. I keep telling the department to replace it, but no one listens to me. A new tube costs six thousand dollars, so they run it to its last breath. Now, if you were in Houston, they would be giving you cobalt. That's real, natural X ray. Stanford likes this, but to me this is artificial X ray. Really, you'd have a better chance if you were getting cobalt."

I am shocked. No one told me prior to treatment that there was a choice between cobalt and the treatment I am getting. "What now?" I ask. "How long before you can fix the machine?"

"Oh, we won't fix it until the last minute," he tells me. "There's probably some life left in it, and this department doesn't waste money. We'll use it until it blows out. I hope there is enough left to complete your treatment today."

Can a tube that is failing deliver an accurate dose? I feel very frightened, but I say nothing.

He leaves the room. Minutes go by before I am reassured by the whirring noise. The machine is on. I count patiently: one, two, up to thirty seconds, half of my treatment. The machine is rotated to my left side. The table is adjusted. It seems to me that I can hear the machine just limp out thirty more seconds.

I fix my collar and prepare to leave. "What happens

now?'' I ask. I am afraid to hear the answer. I don't want my treatment delayed.

''I don't know,'' he replies. ''Only when the tube finally fails will we call for a new one.''

''How long does it take to replace it?''

''Six hours. Don't worry,'' he tells me. ''No one ever completes his treatment in this department without interruption.'' And then he asks, ''What time do you leave from home in the morning?''

''At nine.''

''Okay. I'll call you before nine tomorrow if the machine is down.''

I leave worried and angry, and I resolve to attend the next meeting of the state legislature. I intend to give them hell for shortchanging the medical school. Imagine! The state spends millions, and it's too cheap to spend an extra six thousand for a good tube.

TREATMENT DAY SEVENTEEN

I dawdle this morning. I don't want to leave the house too soon and miss the call from the technician telling me that the machine is down. None comes, so I leave at nine. I am on time, but I am directed to the waiting room.

Waiting in the reception room is a young man who has a tube in his throat to breathe through and uses a slate to write on because he can't talk. I know that's what will happen to me if radiation therapy fails, but it doesn't bother me because my thoughts are all on the tube. Has it blown? Finally the technician calls my name. He greets me, all smiles.

"Tube okay?" I ask anxiously.

"Oh, yeah," he says nonchalantly.

"What happened yesterday?"

"I pressed the wrong button. I hit the emergency button."

The treatment proceeds without incident.

I prepare to leave, and then I begin to complain—but not about his professional carelessness. "You know," I tell him, "you were late starting my treatment today, and I didn't put enough money in the parking meter. I'll probably have a parking fine."

"Sorry," he replies. "Every department in the school has its own budget and its own rules. Other departments pay the fine for you if they have caused the delay, but not this department. I keep telling them that they're wrong and that the patients don't like it, but they won't listen to me. They're too cheap. You're going to have to pay your own fine."

I leave, and I hope that vacations end soon. Of course, it's not only the parking fine I'm concerned about. I wonder if I should report Ted to his superior. His actions have raised doubts in my mind. Have I been getting the right dosage? Is the X-ray beam centered? If he hasn't damaged me physically, he *has* damaged my psyche and made me worry needlessly at a time I should be peaceful.

If a patient reports Ted, his superior can take it as unimportant because it comes from an emotionally disturbed patient. Even if his boss accepts it, the most Ted would get would be a reprimand. But if I report him, that's on a different level; that's colleague talking to colleague, and my complaint cannot be ignored. But no complaints should be ignored. If Ted's unsuited for this work, other people must see it as well as I.

Yet I know the terror of unemployment. When my father came to Omaha, he was employed as a laborer, painting boxcars for the Union Pacific Railroad. His elder brother, Dave, worked as a janitor for the street car company. I was nine when together they had accumulated enough savings to open a men's clothing store, the R.B. Shirt Shop, on Fourteenth and Douglas streets, right in downtown Omaha. First class. They prospered, and shortly thereafter they opened a second store. They continued to prosper, and they achieved the American Dream. There were no restrictive covenants in Omaha, so they bought lots in the best neighborhood, Dundee, near Elmwood Park, and they built new two-story homes in a style then known as Dutch Colonial. There was a separate bedroom for everyone in the family and a garage for a car, which they still did not have.

I was eleven when the bubble burst; they lost their stores, they moved out of their houses, and we moved in with my mother's parents. My father was unemployed, my mother got a sewing machine to make caps, and my brother and I went to work peddling *The Omaha Bee-News* on the streets of the city. I learned what long hours meant: My day in school was from 8:30 to 3:30, peddling papers four to six, Hebrew school from six to eight.

I tasted the panic of what it meant to be unemployed, and ever since then I have been unable to fire anyone. In my practice, I exercised the prerogatives of an older brother and turned the job over to Bill, who proved to be no better at it than I. He eventually turned personnel problems over to the business manager.

I can't report Ted and get him fired. Perhaps . . . probably . . . that is the wrong decision.

TREATMENT DAY EIGHTEEN

On the way to my treatment I meet Dr. Parrin, a competing rheumatologist who is a few years younger than I.

"Ed, what are you doing at the hospital?" he asks.

I admit to him that I have cancer and am getting X-ray therapy.

"Sorry to hear that." He sounds sympathetic. "How are you doing?"

"Well, couldn't be better."

"Don't kid me."

"I'm not kidding."

"Come on, old buddy, you can be honest with me. Tell me the truth."

You bastard, I think, you can't wait to inherit my practice.

When I get home, Dee presents me with some new shirts, and I tell her to return them. Her purchase reminded me of Mr. Stohler, a generous millionaire who died leaving a widow with no children. His will provided that his huge estate be used for the pleasure and comfort of his wife, and on her demise the remainder was to go for the public good.

After a proper mourning period, Mrs. Stohler began to enjoy her wealth. She traveled, she dressed well, she entertained, she enjoyed herself. She lived in this style for many years, and as the years progressed, the estate, under good management, continued to increase. When she reached her eighties, she was a woman of considerable means. Then her life-style changed. She became penurious, refusing to spend any money. She would not allow more than two days' supply of food in the house, nor would she allow her servants to store any household supplies. When the servants protested that they could not keep the house running properly, she insisted that it was important to preserve the estate and there was no need to waste money on things she might never use.

The shirts that Dee bought were nice, and they'd been on sale, but I insisted that she return them to the haberdasher. I didn't expect to need them the following year. I didn't want to waste the money. It seemed sensible to me, not penurious as I had thought Mrs. Stohler was.

TREATMENT DAY NINETEEN

My treatment is at 9:20 A.M. I leave the house before nine and am home by ten. That's my morning's work, and I find that I am too fatigued to do anything else.

Today our three- and six-year-old granddaughters, Jennifer and Lisa, have been left with us. Both of their parents are busy doctors. They watch Grandma Dee Dee solicitously prepare my lunch and set it on the table before me. When Dee refills my coffee cup, Lisa can no longer be quiet. "Papa," she says, "you're a big boy now. You'll have to grow up and learn to make your own lunch."

Ah, women's lib! I lift them both onto my lap and hug them, and they give me kisses. They are bright—at least their grandfather thinks so—and I am happy that they will have opportunities that were denied to my mother because of sex. My fatigue and tension vanish. In my world, grandchildren are terrific medicine.

I am suffering no ill effects, and except for my raspy voice and a little fatigue, it would be hard to know that I am sick. I notice that my family is treating me less and less like a sick man. The initial shock seems to have worn away.

Old people and sick people become eccentric and manipulative because they feel that since they have little time left, they should now have things their way. They go through "the terrible two's" just like little kids. I have often said to women whose husbands have had heart attacks, "I am concerned about you, too. Your husband has gone through a major crisis and is now frightened. He's changed. You will find him irritable, eccentric, and unreasonable."

I have known people to use their illness to manipulate others. I have known mothers who feign illness so that the children would not leave town on vacation. I have known arthritics who deliberately refuse to exercise and thus became wheelchair-bound and dependent.

People can enjoy illness. In Sicily, in World War II, both of my hands were badly burned in a gasoline explosion. They were swathed in bandages so it looked as if I had on boxing gloves. Then I developed diarrhea. There were no toilets, only open-pit latrines in the hot sun. I was miserable. I could not remove my bandages. Yet I did not want to get well. I was delighted to have an honorable reason for not joining my outfit in the combat zone.

At times an illness can almost be welcome. If I could be certain that I was going to recover, life wouldn't be half bad. Everyone is nice to me, no one disagrees with me, no one discusses my diet with me, and I get splendid little gifts.

I have to be very careful not to feel sorry for myself and not to become manipulative. It's not hard for me, I realize suddenly. My life is okay—great family, success, recognition, interesting work. But some people, some of my patients, have terrible troubles. No wonder they're sometimes grateful for permission to lie down awhile and let their burdens go.

TREATMENT DAY TWENTY

I don't want her to come along, but Dee insists on accompanying me this morning. As soon as I was able to go by myself, I would not permit my mother to accompany me to the dentist or to the doctor, and now that I'm married, I don't let my wife come either.

Dee and I got married in Cheyenne, Wyoming, in 1942, right after Pearl Harbor. My outfit was on alert, meaning that we were ready to go on a moment's notice. I wasn't allowed a day off, and we had to get married in the evening after duty hours. There was no time for a proper honeymoon. We moved into a motel room, and a week later I was off on maneuvers in the mountains of Wyoming. That's what our married life was like for five months, and then I was gone for two and a half years. It was only when I returned from the war that I realized that the separation was harder for those who stayed at home than for those who went overseas. I always knew where and how I was. Dee didn't because of censorship. Whenever a major military move was planned, security was accomplished simply by not forwarding the soldiers' mail. Although I wrote frequently, there would be months when she had no news of me. It was only after I came home that I understood how selfish I had been to propose marriage when I was destined to go overseas, and only then did I begin to understand what my absence had meant to Dee.

We have been together for many years, and she is in this cancer boat as much as I am. It is only fair that she go along to the doctor.

At the hospital, Dee is asked to remain in the waiting room. She can't enter the X-ray rooms, and I know that the waiting room isn't going to give her any comfort. She's going to see people without any hair, men who can't talk, and people who are emaciated.

As soon as the treatment is over, the technician calls Dee and escorts both of us into a small examining room. We don't have a long wait for the doctor. He enters, shakes hands with me, says hello to Dee, and then asks the routine questions: How are you? Does your throat hurt? Do you feel tired? Do you have trouble breathing or swallowing? And then he does a quick examination of my skin, apparently not noticing that it is pink. The whole visit is over in five minutes. He is so quick, so solemn and uncommunicative, that I realize that Dee isn't going to get much comfort from this visit. I'm embarrassed, in a way, that she sees what short shrift I get from a colleague.

We drive home without speaking. We are both probably thinking the same thing: Will we be together this time next year?

TREATMENT DAY TWENTY-ONE

The treatment is routine. The problem arises when I return home. Anna, who does housework for us, is out of sorts. An Asian refugee, she is short, round, and usually jolly. When I ask her what her problem was, she tells me, "I've got a stomach cancer."

"Have you been sick?" I ask.

"No."

"Do you have heartburn or indigestion?"

"No."

"Then why do you think you have stomach cancer?"

"I don't know, the doctor just said so."

"Did he Xray you?"

"No."

"Did he stick a tube with a light down your stomach?"

"No."

"It doesn't make sense to me," I tell her.

"I don't know," she says, "but I'm going to have an operation next week."

I let the matter drop, but her story doesn't add up.

Later in the day she reopens the conversation. "Were you scared when they told you you had cancer?"

"Terribly. I still am."

"So am I," Anna confides.

"Would you like to have me call your doctor?" I ask.

"Yes, please. Call Dr. Gold."

I think that Bill Gold, like most doctors, will resent

my butting in. After all, what right do I have? I'm not her doctor. But he is respectful and cooperative.

"I don't remember telling Anna that she has stomach cancer," he tells me. "I did a Pap smear. She has a localized cancer of the cervix."

"Her outlook is good?"

"We don't plan any Xray, only a local excision."

"Why does she think she has stomach cancer?"

"I don't know," Gold says. Then he hesitates for a while. "You know what I think happened? I probably told her that if the cancer had spread, we would have had to open her stomach—I meant abdomen, of course, but I thought she wouldn't understand."

Such misunderstandings occur often and cause needless suffering. The first year of medical school is spent learning a new language that makes students feel special and important. Thereafter, for the rest of their lives, instead of speaking plain English, doctors use words like hemoptysis to mean spitting up blood and emesis to mean vomiting. The problem becomes worse as they advance in their training. By the time they are residents and interns, they begin to use abbreviations such as COPE, which means chronic, obstructive, pulmonary emphysema. Doctors have so many of these abbreviations that they have even had to develop dictionaries that define these terms.

All my life I have listened to practitioners saying one thing and patients hearing another. When I was in medical school a bright ten-year-old girl was admitted because of diabetes. She was so uncooperative that the frustrated staff could not deal with her. In desperation, a psychologist was brought to see her.

He explained the problem to the staff. "The child was sure she was dying. She had heard her doctor describing her case to the students, and when she heard him say that she had diabetes, she interpreted it to mean she would 'die of beeties.' "

From that time on I was very conscious of the need to be careful. But I was not always successful. One patient, a young eighteen-year-old, once called me. "Am I going to die?" she asked.

"I don't know. What makes you think you're dying?"

"When I was in the office today you put your arms around me and said, 'Good-bye, old friend.' You never did that before."

I assured her that she had misinterpreted my gesture and that I had only meant to be friendly.

At my first visit, when Dr. DuVall had told me I had cancer, he'd shaken my hand and said, "I'm sorry to meet you under these circumstances." At that time, I'd taken his expression to mean that he was saying good-bye—a final good-bye—when in fact what he was doing was expressing sympathy. I used to think a little condescendingly about patients who misinterpret doctors' words and expressions. Yet, with all my experience, I did the same. Patients are vulnerable. They need good, plain language to explain their situations. Even so, they are watching for every sign from the doctor. Maybe there's nothing much to be done about that, but a spoonful of empathy might help.

TREATMENT DAY TWENTY-TWO

My third son, Howard, with his wife, Marcia, and their one-year-old son, Sam, come for a short visit. Howard and Marcia are psychiatrists in San Francisco. I view their visit with suspicion, as a duty call. Many people have asked me whether they should travel to visit a dying parent. Why do you have to call a doctor to ask if you should visit a dying relative? I always listen to their reasons for going or not going and advise them to make their own decision.

Howard offers to drive me to the hospital for my treatment, and I consent because it eliminates the parking problem. Sam climbs into the car with us to sit on his father's lap, pretending to drive. It wasn't too long ago that Howard did that with me.

Sam is named after my father, who has been dead three years. The baby's sweatshirt says "Sam Rosenbaum," and I am startled to read it. When I look at the child, I see my father, whom he looks like. I wonder about reincarnation. To my way of thinking, we are four generations in that car: my dad Sam, the new Sam, my son Howard, and myself.

The road from my house to the hospital winds through forested hills, and Howard and I are silent. I remember driving this road so often on the way to school or to Little League or hospital rounds, when Howard and the other boys were children. Howard must be thinking of the hundreds of times he drove it during four difficult years in medical school. Sam chatters with excitement at seeing the woods, the sun through the trees, and the curving road.

When we arrive at the hospital, Howard suggests that he and Sam drive around for fifteen minutes while I have my treatment. But today is different. The therapy department is behind schedule. It's at least half an hour before I come back outside. Howard and Sam are waiting patiently. No one scolds me because I am late. Why did I get so anxious? I get into the car, and Sam climbs into my lap and plants a big kiss on the top of my bald head. I hold him very close.

I want to be around for his second birthday. I know that emotions and willpower can have a lot to do with the course of a disease. When it comes to cancer, I suspect that the psyche has very little effect, but I am determined to do my best.

TREATMENT DAY TWENTY-THREE

I can no longer ignore my skin. It is getting a deeper tan, and I don't have to shave in the area that is being treated. I finally give in and call the technician's attention to changes that are going on.

"Yes," she says, "the hair follicles have been destroyed, probably permanently, and the burn goes all the way down to your vocal cords, but your skin is not over-reacting, and I think you will be able to complete your treatments. In some patients, we have to stop or delay treatment because of skin reactions."

I feel better after hearing that. I don't want anything to interfere with my completing the treatment, because I know if that happens, the statistical odds are not in my favor.

Driving home, I think about Dee. I have known wives to dread their husbands' retirement because they can't stand the idea of them being around the house all day. Now it is happening to Dee and me. I am tired, I can't talk, all I do is eat, sleep, and sit around the house. I wonder how she's taking it.

When I get home, I grab Dee, squeeze her and give her a kiss, like the first one I gave her when she was twenty-two. She responds, but I can taste the tears on her cheeks.

"Don't worry," I assure her, "I'll be all right. When this is over we'll take a trip, maybe a cruise."

"Okay," she says, "only be sure that the ship has cabins with double beds."

For the first time in a month I laugh and I hug her hard, knowing how lucky I am to have her.

TREATMENT DAY TWENTY-FOUR

S he often arrives when I do, this attractive, neatly dressed woman who covers her hair with a bandana. They always call me in first, so she has the advantage—she knows my name. Usually we greet each other and respect each other's privacy, but today she starts a conversation.

"I know you. We met at a medical meeting. I'm Tim Duggin's wife from Medford."

"I remember you now," I say. "What are you being treated for?"

"Brain tumor."

"How did they find it?"

"I had a seizure. The doctor ordered a CAT scan, but because they had had a death from the iodine injection and because I'm allergic to shellfish, they skipped the iodine."

"What's the use of doing the X ray if you don't inject the iodine?"

"You're right," she answers. "The CAT scan was reported as normal. I was started on phenobarbital and Tegretol. Two months later I collapsed at a meeting in Portland. A repeat CAT scan, this time with iodine, showed the tumor. Dr. Kettle operated. The tumor was too close to vital structures for removal, so I'm getting Xray.''

"Cobalt?"

"No, the linear accelerator, the same as you. My tumor is grade IV. Kettle is not very optimistic.''

"Oh, he can't be certain. I had a patient with a similar diagnosis. All the experts shook their heads. It's now eight years. He's alive, well, married, holds a good job, has a wife, and they've just had a baby.''

"That makes me feel better," she says.

"You seem to be taking it well."

"I am. The thing that bothers me most is losing my hair,'' she says, smiling.

"Let that be the least of your troubles. Look at me. I'm bald, and I'm making it.''

Calmly she opens her book. She is reading the psalms.

But I don't feel calm. Because I see her so often and because we are in the same boat, I feel like her brother and I am upset with the way she's been treated. Her doctor made a grievous error in the management of her case. The risk of a serious reaction to the iodine injection was remote. His failure to perform the procedure properly resulted in a missed and delayed diagnosis of cancer. There's a good chance my companion won't make it . . . because of a stupid medical decision.

I have had many doctors and their families as patients. It started early in my career, when a sixty-year-old physician selected me to do his annual physical examination. We had met at a hospital breakfast, and he must have been impressed by my youth and training. I was flattered. I had plenty of time to do a good examination, but instead of going through a thorough and careful history, we spent most of the time in the cafeteria chatting over coffee. After all, I thought, he's a doctor. I don't have to ask him embarrassing questions; he'd know what to tell me if there were any problems.

Two days later he died in his office of a heart attack. I

would not have missed the diagnosis if I had done a careful history. From that day on I treated medical families like ordinary patients. There were no exceptions. I insisted that I write all prescriptions, that they report any changes to me, and that they make regular appointments.

Even these precautions did not always suffice. Dr. Hamstead asked me to see his wife when she developed rheumatoid arthritis. She was a new mother, only thirty years old, and already she seemed old. She would get up in the morning stiff and sore, her swollen hands looked like sausages, and she was tired before the day had begun.

An intelligent woman, Mrs. Hamstead seemed to grasp everything that I was telling her—the importance of physical and emotional rest and a regular program of physiotherapy. Then I prescribed aspirin. I explained to her that in the early stages of the disease, common aspirin is the drug of choice, but it was important that this simple medication be taken in measured and proper doses. And then to be certain there were no errors, I wrote out her instructions:

"Aspirin, three every four hours,
or
if your stomach is upset, try coated aspirin,
or
if you prefer, take buffered aspirin, three every four hours."

My handwriting is the typical doctor's script, unreadable, and so I printed the instructions. And then, to be sure she understood, I read them to her.

When she returned in a week, I was delighted by what I saw. Her hands were no longer swollen. She assured me that she felt well, but she acted punch-drunk. Her blood tests showed dangerously high levels of aspirin in her body. What had happened? She had misinterpreted my instructions. Every four hours she had taken three

regular aspirin, *plus* three coated aspirin, *plus* three buffered aspirin. She must have missed some doses, or she
never would have been able to walk into my office.

TREATMENT DAY TWENTY-FIVE

T oday is doctor's day again, and it's very much like
the previous visits. Hello-how-are-you, a quick feel
of my neck, and good-bye.

I am beginning to understand the patient's frustration
with my profession: twenty-five dollars or more for a
quick hello and good-bye. But I also understand the doctor. When a physician sees twenty to thirty patients a
day, day after day, it all becomes routine. He depends on
the patient to call attention to problems, and the patient
is afraid to say anything for fear of upsetting the great
man. And then there are questions we all avoid asking
because we're afraid of the answer: "I don't know." Who
wants a doctor who doesn't know?

TREATMENT DAY TWENTY-SIX

I arrive at nine this morning, and the waiting room is
empty.
"Not busy today?" I ask.

"You should have been here a few minutes ago," the receptionist answers.

"What time do you start?"

"Seven A.M."

"Seven? Why so early?"

"So some of our patients can go back to work. We have one man who drives fifty miles from Salem. He leaves home at six and is back at work by eight."

I feel guilty. I haven't worked since I started treatment.

In the treatment room the technician greets me. "Your treatment will take a little longer today. First we'll take an X ray of your larynx to see if we've been hitting the target."

"I thought everything was fixed on Day One when you set the machines and tattooed me."

"Yes," she explains, "but sometimes with weight loss and time, the tattoo marks shift."

What is she talking about? This whole thing is crazy and out of control. If my tattoo marks have shifted, it means they have been aiming at the wrong target. They have been missing my vocal cords and the site of my cancer. But they can't go back and correct the error because my skin has already taken the maximum dose of X-ray it can safely tolerate. And so I say, "What good will it do to know? You can't give me any more Xray to correct the error. Right?"

"Right, but if we're off target, at least we'll know why we failed."

She snaps the picture. "You'll have to wait until Dr. Reed checks these before I can treat you," she says and leaves the room.

I lie frozen on the hard table. I close my eyes to block out reality. I try to concentrate on my patients, my wife, my grandchildren. Not much luck. Time passes slowly, slowly, slowly.

Finally she returns. "On target," she says cheerily and proceeds with the treatment.

I am very angry with my doctors. What good would it do now to know that they have been missing the target? I don't understand why they didn't run a check early in the treatment. This check is being done not for my benefit but for future statistics, to determine why they failed with me.

Yet I don't want to upset them because I know that most doctors have a need to be respected and loved by their patients. They have trouble dealing with hostility when it surfaces. The experienced physician is aware that bad news can generate anger. Instead of saying bluntly that a patient has high blood pressure or a stomach ulcer, the doctor might say, "You have a disease of bankers' high blood pressure," or, "Like most important executives, you have an ulcer."

Every medical student dreams of the day when he or she will enter private practice and make a brilliant diagnosis. The patient will have seen scores of other doctors who have been mystified by the strange disease, but the medical student on his first day of practice will outshine them all. He will make the diagnosis, the patient will be eternally grateful, the new doctor's reputation will be established, and his success will be assured. Real life is not like that. Patients are not particularly happy or grateful, particularly if the diagnosis is bad or the prognosis is poor.

In my early days of practice, I was flattered when the chief of the hospital staff invited me to lunch—just the two of us. Then, over lunch, I learned the reason why: a wealthy, important patient of his had an undiagnosed illness. Maybe I, as a new young doctor just out of training, could help.

The chief spent the entire lunch hour detailing the patient's illness. As I listened, I was exhilarated. My dreams were about to be fulfilled. I knew the answer already. I knew because I had trained at the Mayo Clinic and had seen similar cases from all over the world.

The patient had Buerger's disease, a rare condition that affects the arteries and veins of the extremities. Untreated, it can lead to gangrene and loss of a limb. It was first described by Dr. Buerger and was initially thought to be limited to Jewish males, but by this time we knew that it affected all races and religions. Because Buerger had done all his work at Mt. Sinai Hospital in New York, all his patients were Jewish—hence the original error.

I visited the patient in the hospital that evening. I spent very little time on the history. After all, I had spent a whole lunch hour on that. A quick physical examination confirmed my suspicions, and I informed the patient of the diagnosis.

Modestly I related the story to Dee that evening. "Today I made a diagnosis of Buerger's disease in a powerful, important executive. Other doctors missed it. My reputation is made. I am a success. Tomorrow my office will be full of patients."

I was wrong. I never had a referral from the patient, nor did I see him again. Months later his wife came in to pay his bill.

"What happened?" I asked.

"I'm embarrassed to tell you," she said. "He refused to pay your bill. I'm paying this out of my personal account."

"He must be awfully stingy."

"No," she went on, "he hates you. He says that before you came along, he saw the best doctors in town. None of them knew the answer, yet you, in five minutes, made the diagnosis. He says like all Jews you're much too smart, and even worse, you gave him a Jewish diagnosis. He has no Jewish ancestry. He refuses to pay your bill, and he will never see you again."

TREATMENT DAY TWENTY-SEVEN

T he waiting room has three boxes. One box has toys for the children. The second has current reading material—not bad for a doctor's office. The third rack has American Cancer Society literature. I have avoided reading the latter, but today I am optimistic. I gingerly take one of the pamphlets, the one on breast cancer. To me that's the safest. I peek through it. It's not too threatening. Nothing there that can hurt me. As I read the article on radiation therapy, I understand more clearly that there are many forms of X rays, that in addition to those naturally occurring, there are man-made rays, some the result of atomic research, that have not yet been tried in cancer therapy.

Finally I have enough courage to read the pamphlet on cancer of the larynx. It says that 85 percent of all patients are alive five years after therapy. Seventy-five percent are alive ten years after therapy. So where does that leave me? What sense can I make of these figures? For example, the life expectancy for a man my age is nine more years. But these statistics say I have a 75 percent chance of being alive in ten years, so does that mean I will live longer because of my throat cancer?

I ponder how to interpret statistics. In World War II, I landed with the First Division at Oran in North Africa. Months after the invasion we received newspapers from home. One headline read, "Americans Lose under 100 Men in the African Invasion." That's true, I thought, but for that hundred men and their families, the mortality was 100 percent. Now, which statistics apply to me?

When I get home, Aunt Emma is waiting for me. Emma has a reputation for nonstop talk, and today she lives up to her reputation. Because my voice is gone, all I can do is nod or shake my head at appropriate intervals. Finally she looks at her watch and apologizes, "I didn't realize how late it was."

I accompany her to the door. "You know," she says, "this is the best conversation you and I have ever had."

I've had other one-sided conversations. When I first met one patient, Alvin Coll, he was fifty-five, with the weathered face of an outdoor laborer. His most striking feature was his cleft palate, and his speech was so impaired that I had difficulty understanding him. His examinations and tests were normal, and it was only after four visits that I finally comprehended that he was short of breath and had chest pain on exertion or with emotional stress. Based on his history, I determined that he had heart disease, angina pectoris, and I prescribed nitroglycerin tablets.

After I had been caring for him for a year he said, "Doctor, thanks to you I am well. The advice you gave me did it."

I was stumped. "What did I tell you to do?"

"I sold the farm, just as you told me to."

I never knew he owned a farm.

TREATMENT DAY TWENTY-EIGHT

Today in the X-ray department there is a notice: No TREATMENT MONDAY, LABOR DAY. Another delay. I'm supposed to get thirty treatments. If they gave me one every day, my ordeal would be over in four weeks, but weekends and holiday vacations stretch my therapy over six weeks.

Problems like this may seem unimportant, but as a physician I know the possible consequences to the patient of the staff holiday and the delay in treatment that results. Now, for the first time since my illness, I have the courage to read some texts on laryngeal cancer. One author recommends that cancer of the vocal cords be treated by surgery, not by X ray. I wish now that I hadn't read it. Most patients accept their doctors' recommendations without question, though this has changed in recent years. I did the same for a long time, but what troubles me is that I know better.

Even the most distinguished scientists make serious mistakes. In 1940 the Nobel Prize for Medicine was given to a surgeon who introduced prefrontal lobotomy for schizophrenia. As the years went on, we found that those patients who were operated on were helped only temporarily and then were much worse off than patients who had never been treated. Today, if a doctor dared to perform such an operation, he would deserve to be tarred and feathered and run out of town.

Doctors keep changing their minds. Treatments, like fashion, change from season to season. For a generation estrogen, the female hormone, was used to alleviate the symptoms of menopause. Then estrogen went out of style, for it was feared that it could cause breast or uterine cancer. Now it is again coming back in vogue because a lack of estrogen may cause osteoporosis, or softening of the bones. In one issue of one of our most prestigious medical journals there are two articles on estrogen. One, written by experts, proves that estrogen causes heart disease, while the other, written by equally prestigious experts, proves that estrogen prevents heart disease.

Now I am confused. Should I be getting X-ray therapy or should I have had surgery? I can't blame it on my doctors. I never raised any questions. And if I had, how could I have reached a logical decision? And I'm a trained person. Think of the problem it must be for the layperson.

I am confused, and I have done the same thing to some of my patients. When Mary Dove consulted me, I prescribed estrogen. She questioned my decision, which aggravated me.

She had described her symptoms to me: she had hot flashes, cried readily, and had mood swings, all symptoms typical of the menopause. I knew of no better treatment than the female hormone, but newspaper stories and articles in women's magazines were addressing the problems of estrogen. Patients were becoming rebellious, they dared to ask questions.

Mary Dove's response to the prescription was, "I don't think I should take it. I've read that hormones cause cancer."

"I know about the reports," I replied, "but you've had a hysterectomy, so you don't have to worry about cancer of the uterus, and breast cancer is a remote possibility. Meanwhile, you're suffering, and I don't know of anything else that will help."

"I don't know." She hesitated and did not take the prescription.

I started to leave the room, thought about the problem, and then handed her the prescription again, saying, "Look, it's what I give my own wife. Now will you take it?"

"No," she emphatically replied.

"Why?"

"You could be making a mistake with her as well as with me. And anyway, how do I know what you think of your wife?"

There *were* a lot of unresolved questions about the use of estrogen. There still are. Why was I so sure that the patient was wrong?

Now I, too, am getting conflicting signals about my treatment, and there isn't much I can do about it. I have already started my X-ray treatment, and there is no turning back.

LABOR DAY WEEKEND

SUNDAY

Sunday night I can no longer tolerate the boredom of this life I'm leading, so we go to the movies, where we encounter Dr. Russ Cass, a urologist about fifteen years my junior. I would like to avoid him, but he sees me first.

"Dr. Ed," he shouts across the lobby, "how are you? I haven't seen you around the hospital."

My voice gives my secret away, so I have to admit my problem. Then I whisper, "Why the Dr. Ed? Just call me Ed."

"Oh, I couldn't do that, you're much too authoritative a figure for me to be familiar with. I can't call you anything but Doctor. I still remember my student days when you were one of the great teachers."

Pure bull, I think, he wants me to refer some cases to him. But I don't say what I think. Instead I ask, "Such as?"

He hesitates, then answers, "Some of the things I remember best are: first, do no harm; if you don't know what's wrong, don't treat; if the patient demands treatment and there is no treatment, practice skillful neglect. And I've never forgotten this one: 'Eighty to ninety percent of the patients would get well without ever seeing a doctor or taking medicine.' "

"All generic stuff," I answer, "nothing original, words that every lecturer uses."

"Maybe, but I still remember your lecture on unexpected and delayed side effects of drugs. That was a classic."

The movie starts, ending our conversation, but the picture is so dull it doesn't take my mind off myself. I think about Dr. Cass. He was an average student, yet he has done well in practice. Patients like him because he is jolly, gregarious, and optimistic. His colleagues refer cases to him, not because he is the best doctor but for the same reasons his patients selected him. To referring doctors he is friendly, complimentary, and nonthreatening. He has the knack of always being the first to grab for the restaurant check, and his Christmas gifts are generous.

But this time his style has backfired. He has reminded me of my lectures on drug toxicity, and that is one subject I prefer not to think about. It is impossible to predict in advance which patient will react adversely to a drug, since every person is biologically unique. For example, I had a patient who died from one aspirin tablet, only because he was uniquely allergic.

Most medical students become hypochondriacs. I never

had that problem myself, but when it came to my children, I always imagined the worst and often was guilty of starting treatment prematurely. When second son Jim was five, he developed a fever. At that time I was foolish enough to treat my own family. Jim did not respond to penicillin, so I gave him a newer antibiotic, chloramphenicol. My boy recovered, but during that same period Dr. Karr, a colleague, gave his five-year-old son the same drug. The boy died. The drug destroyed his bone marrow.

At this time I am not worried about the short-term side effects of the X-ray treatment. I have made it, I am almost through. What concerns me now are the long-term effects. What will happen to me in the future because of my treatment? Man was not created to take medicine. Drugs and medical procedures may have delayed or unknown side effects. It's as if the gods eventually demand payment for our interference in the natural course of life.

Aspirin has been used since 1898, and millions of tons have been dispensed. For generations parents have treated their babies' colds and fevers with aspirin. Only in this generation have we learned that this can be a dangerous practice. Only now do we know that in some few cases aspirin given to children with fever may cause a fatal disease.

Rheumatoid arthritis, my specialty, is a difficult disease to treat. A drug may help the first patient and do nothing for the next. In the 1960s cyclophosphamide, a drug used to treat blood cancer, was tried for rheumatoid arthritis with excellent results. Cases that up to that point had not responded to anything responded to this new treatment. The problem was that a few years later some of these patients cured of arthritis died of cancer caused by the cyclophosphamide treatment.

Sometimes a drug given to one generation may affect a future generation. Years ago, mothers who threatened to abort were given a drug called diethylstilbestrol, or DES. When their daughters were born, they were normal, healthy babies, but as these children approached their teens, many of them developed genital cancer from the estrogen given to their mothers.

The question in my mind today is this: if I survive and the X-ray treatment cures my cancer, will I die later of another disease caused by the X ray?

No one can answer that question, but I know from my experience that there are no free rides. We violate a principle of nature when we interrupt the natural course of a disease.

MONDAY

There are three days with no treatment over the Labor Day holiday, and I feel abandoned. Portland is deserted. Everyone has gone to the beach or to the mountains. In summer our weather is perfect—warm, dry, sunny days and cool nights—but after Labor Day, when the autumn rains begin, there will be many wet, cloudy days and little sun until next summer.

All our friends and family have left the city for their last flings. The Oregon coast is only ninety minutes away. There the days are in the cool seventies, the mornings are misty, the surf pounds against the rocks. I could stroll the sand beaches and feast in numerous little seaside restaurants on fresh Dungeness crab or the local razor clams. I would be there with my family if it weren't for my illness.

Because I am feeling so restless, I ask Dee to go with me for a drive. Our house is ten minutes from downtown Portland, but it is as if we live in the country; we are surrounded by tall firs in a hilly, forested area. As we drive to the city center, we descend a thousand feet along a curving narrow roadway that offers us vistas of snow-covered mountains, and we can look down on the heart of the city, bisected by the Willamette River. Because of the holiday, there is little traffic on the streets. Even on workdays, we are not accustomed to big-city traffic, but today in particular the city seems deserted. I don't encounter ten cars between my house and the downtown area. In the city center, I can park where I like. A lone city bus drives along the Mall, and there are some sightseeing buses parked in front of the hotels, but there are few pedestrians on the street and the stores are closed.

I have a strong urge to see my office. I haven't been there in six weeks. The street is as deserted as downtown. My office is a one-story brick building, and next door is a restaurant, Rose's, founded by my mother-in-law. I feel a lurch of nostalgia and wonder if I will ever be able to come back. For thirty years, every workday, I have had lunch at Rose's; even after my mother-in-law sold the restaurant, the new proprietor still reserved a table for my office. It is one of the few places in town where you can get a corned beef sandwich or a bowl of matzo ball soup. At lunch I am joined by my brother, my sons, my nephews, and my partners. Our lunches are simple. What is important is the comradery and the conversation. We discuss our problem cases, someone offers the joke of the day. No one raises his voice, arguments are unknown; it's not the Rosenbaum style. I preside over all this as the proud patriarch. How many men in this world can sit in peace with their brothers, their sons, his nephews, and their partners? And now, so suddenly, it seems to be all over.

TREATMENT DAY TWENTY-NINE

I have almost completed my treatment, but instead of getting less apprehensive, I am more tense than ever. When I was told that I had cancer, I went into a state of shock. When the doctor tried to reassure me, I thought to myself, "Don't kid me! That's what I say when I have to tell the bad news to my patients. Even when I know that they are going to die, I offer hope and treatment."

As the days have passed, I have recovered from the shock and have been lulled by the daily ritual. My voice deteriorated to the point where I could only whisper. I took to wearing a police whistle tied to a cord around my neck so that I could respond when Dee called me. I have not seen Dr. DuVall, who made the diagnosis, since the surgery. The radiologist, Dr. Reed, sees me once a week but spends little time with me. But the day of reckoning is near, and I dread being reexamined and hearing the words, "The X ray didn't work; we'll have to operate." Like a defendant in a trial, I am getting so close to the time when the jury will come in with a verdict. No wonder I am tense. No one says anything to me, and the Labor Day holiday's interrupting my treatment has added to my discomfort.

Now it's the day after Labor Day, and I have returned to the hospital to resume my therapy. During the summer the hospital halls were deserted. Now they are full. Little knots of students stand around chattering. I recognize them as juniors because they wear white jackets with stethoscopes hung around their necks.

Today is their first contact with the real thing—the live patient! As they get onto the elevator I listen to their conversation.

"Did you see his icteric sclera?"

"His bilirubin must be up."

"He's not a drinker."

"I'll bet it's CA."

The students seem enchanted with their facility with the new vocabulary they've acquired that says the guy is jaundiced, he's not a drinker, and he probably has cancer of the liver. To them, it's very new and very exciting. To the patient, it's frightening.

* * *

Though it's been many years since I was a student, I remember how proud I was of that white coat and stethoscope. Our first two years had been spent in the laboratory with books and animals. In our junior year we were allowed on the wards to be with the patients. Then we were initiated into the secrets of the exclusive, honored profession. Medical education at that time was directed toward making the diagnosis; treatment was given much less emphasis. If the patient died, we strove to get permission from the family for an autopsy. The student who got the most permissions received an award.

The examination of the body tissues after death is the definitive way to determine the correct diagnosis. In those days, even the best doctors expected to be wrong half the time. Modern autopsy studies show that, in the best hospitals, good physicians miss the diagnosis in one patient out of four, and in one case out of ten the patient would have survived if the right diagnosis had been made. In some hospitals, the magnitude of error can be as high as 40 percent, no better than we used to do in my early days. The use of modern diagnostic techniques has not eliminated the need for the physician's good judgment. Overreliance on some of these procedures may give a false sense of security and lead to missed diagnoses.

Early in medical school a doctor learns that he cannot know it all; the field is too vast and complicated, and some mistakes are inevitable. The hope is that you won't repeat them. The doctor who never acknowledges a mistake is a dangerous fool.

Lucy Candrel taught me my lesson. She was a middle-aged woman who complained of muscle pain, joint swelling, and fatigue. I followed her for five years, and I suspected that she had systemic lupus erythematosus. But the problem in diagnosing that disease is that laboratory tests can be positive one day and negative the next. I had made the diagnosis primarily on what the patient said and not on solid laboratory evidence. She responded to cortisone, the standard treatment, but taken over a long period of time the drug has serious side effects. Every time I would try to withdraw or reduce the dose, Lucy would resist. I worried about her. I was giving her a toxic drug, I wasn't a hundred percent certain of the diagnosis, and I could not stop her treatment.

As time went on, the patient began to complain of more pain. I refused to give her more cortisone, for that would have killed her. I denied her codeine, because if narcotics are used to treat chronic pain, addiction develops.

One night I got a call from the hospital emergency room. Lucy was there demanding pain pills. "Admit her," I instructed.

She spent the next week in the hospital having numerous X rays and laboratory tests and seeing consultants. There was no evidence of disease. One morning on rounds, I presented her case to the students, and I told the young doctors, "This is a good example of how a patient can have no disease and fool even the best doctors, all resulting in overtreatment." However, I decided to cover all bases. I had planned to send her home the next day, but I ordered a bone scan, a test in which radioactive material is injected into the veins and deposited into the bones.

The radiologist called that afternoon: "The bone scan shows widespread cancer in her pelvis and spine."

Lucy didn't live much longer. The autopsy showed a very small, undetected breast cancer that had not enlarged in the breast but had broken away and seeded the skeletal system.

Despite all I know, now that I am the patient, I want my physician to be God. I want to believe that the doctor knows all.

A patient once introduced himself to me with the following speech: "I have rheumatoid arthritis. I have searched the world for the best doctors. I was surprised when I wrote to the American Rheumatoid Association and they referred me to you. Your office is only a block from my house!"

"To be honest with you," I told him, "if I had your disease, even the best doctor in the world wouldn't be good enough for me."

The fact is that even though I've got a pretty good reputation in my field, I have never *cured* anyone of arthritis. I've helped people, sure, but there were cases where my patients were in constant, intractable pain and there was little I could do for them. So, now, in my own case, do I have the best doctor in the world for my condition? Who knows? And even if he is the best, can he help me?

I try to take my mind off my own problems by thinking of the students. I wonder if these students are as good as my classmates. In my time there were three applications for every medical school admission slot; now there are less than two applicants for each opening.

Women used to be a rarity in medical school. It was a closed fraternity. There were no girls in my class; most of them had been shunted to nursing. Few medical schools had more than three or four women students, and those who were admitted to medical school often suffered harassment.

It was the rule in those days to fail 25 percent of the freshman class. In my class, 104 entered, seventy-two graduated. The flunk course was anatomy. In some medical schools, the opening lecture was by the anatomy professor. The stock lecture was to tell the students what a miserable life they were going to face for the next four years, and then the girl in the class got special attention: she would be put to work dissecting the penis.

By the time I entered practice, there were five or six women in a class of a hundred. After I became chief of the rheumatology clinic, I began to offer a summer scholarship to students. The one selected would work with me in my office, and now that I think about it, most of the time I selected a woman. In my lifetime of practice, I have had six partners, three of whom were women. One of these partners once remarked to me, "You know, you and your brother both like girls." And I thought, Who doesn't? But I don't think that was the entire reason; I think it was something that my mother ingrained in me. So often I would hear her say, "I wish I could have been a doctor." I must have passed on some of what I felt to my sons, for three of them married professional working women, one a lawyer and two of them doctors.

Today 35 to 50 percent of the entering medical school class are women. The fail rate is 1 or 2 percent, and I hope that the harassment is gone. It's all for the better.

Still, I wonder how to select medical students, male or female? At random? Should we ignore scientific abilities and pick those who will be most sympathetic, or should we chose the withdrawn academic who will be unable to relate to the patient?

These students are from a new and very different generation. To my father, it was acceptable to work sixteen hours a day, seven days a week. To me, a fourteen-hour day with night calls thrown in was the norm. The new crop of doctors demands a twelve-hour day with vacations and days off. They are right: long hours lead to fatigue and errors in judgment. On the other hand, when doctors change shifts, patients are often subject to needless reexamination and errors. The students want relief from the stress of overwork, but their solution—more time off—isn't good for the patient. When one of my patients developed a complication, I didn't sleep at night; the truth is that I hope these young doctors will suffer in the same way.

Are they as good as my generation? Probably yes. There are ninety students in the class; a few can walk on water, the rest will be acceptable, and there will be a few who graduate who never should have started medicine. The worry is that the pool of acceptable candidates is shrinking. The good students are being enticed away from medicine by computer science, business, and law, where the pay is higher. If this continues, the quality of medical care will deteriorate.

How will the public know the difference? I did a poor job of selecting my own doctors. I chose them because they were friends. Now, with the wisdom of hindsight, I could make a better choice. First, I would be concerned with integrity. The blindest purchase we make in our life is medical care. We have no basis of comparison. So I want my doctor to have integrity. I want to be sure that his advice is for my benefit and not for his—or hers.

Next, I would want to know about the doctor's knowledge. What school did he graduate from? Where was his residency? Does he have specialty boards? Has he kept up? What do his colleagues think of him? What is his track record in treating my illness?

Only after these questions are answered would I concern myself with questions of personality. Is he sympathetic? Does he listen? Does he communicate? Are we compatible? Sympathy is high on my list, but what good is sympathy if the doctor doesn't have knowledge? Are any of my doctors sympathetic? I don't even know. I have precious little contact with them. Have I been sympathetic to my patients? A few months ago I would have answered with a firm "yes." Now I'm beginning to see that more may be required than I gave.

Doctors talk of empathy. Some practitioners have it, some don't; I don't think it's something that can be learned. I prided himself on my ability to relate to even the most difficult patients. Many physicians ask disruptive sufferers to seek help elsewhere. I never did. If the ill person was difficult to manage, I always assumed that it was my fault. A sick person is anxious and worried; I was well. The one who had to make the adjustment was me, and I always tried to do that.

Arthur Brown, a Portland attorney, came from a family that always shouted. He was convinced that that was the way to intimidate his opponents. He did well in the courtroom, but the doctors in town hated him because he was so unreasonable and demanding. He came to see me only because he had been unable to get along with his previous doctors. His problem—a common cold. He was in my office in the morning, and by lunchtime he was shouting over the phone, "I saw you this morning, I paid your goddamn bill in cash, and I still have a cold."

I stayed calm. "We're like lawyers," I said, "we need a little time."

He laughed and made an appointment for his mother. She was worse than he, but we got along so well I was invited to her eightieth birthday party.

When my nephew, Bob, first joined our practice, I assigned him one of my patients. He spent an hour with her and then came out of the room perspiring. "I can't get anywhere with her, Uncle Ed," he told me. "I don't know why you put up with her."

I went into the patients' room and spent a few minutes calming her down. She was smiling when she went into the hallway but frowned at Bob. "Why can't you be like your uncle?" she asked him. "It only took him a few minutes to tell me what was wrong."

Bob laughed later about my "charisma," which I suppose was his way of saying I could relate; I could sympathize; I could understand. But now that I have been a patient, I know that you can't really understand unless you have been there yourself. I thought that I was good, but now I know that I wasn't good enough. Today I would be better.

Doctors are dedicated to helping people, yet the students in the elevator with me are getting their kicks from someone else's misery, concentrating, as usual, on the diagnosis, not on how the patient feels.

Once when I was a sophomore in medical school, eighty of us sat in rows in the amphitheater. In a bed on center stage lay a big, burly farmer from western Nebraska. He was completely naked, his upper torso exposed, his lower half covered with a sheet. The professor described the patient's heart murmur. Then eighty students lined up, each with his new stethoscope, and listened to the heart. The sounds were so new and strange to them that most of them only pretended to hear the murmur. The farmer lay patiently as each student passed by. When the last one was finished, he jumped from his bed, standing completely nude, and vented his rage. "Goddamn it," he shouted, "I came to this hospital seven days ago to have my hemorrhoids operated on! Now when are you guys going to do the job?"

I walk slowly toward the X-ray department. I know it will be a long time before the young doctors can understand what the diagnosis of cancer means to their patients. When I arrive at the appointment desk the therapist is ready for me. Because I've grown accustomed to the treatments, today I don't close my eyes when I lay down on the table. Instead, I watch the huge ball of the X-ray machine above me. It rotates around my head, first from right to left, then from left to right, and as it rotates I can see that it has a hole in the middle. The ball reminds me of a giant's eye, and the whole machine begins to take on the aspect of a living giant. I look at the eye with fear, for it is through the hole in the eye that the deadly X-ray beam emanates. As the machine starts to whir, generating beams, I try to shut out what I have seen. For near the machine's iris is the manufacturer's nameplate. The machine is old! There are other, perhaps better, and certainly newer, more expensive models, the kind they would have used had I gone to Mayo, or Stanford, or Sloan-Kettering. I'd have been away from home for six weeks, but Dee could have come with me. And now it's too late. There's only one treatment to go!

TREATMENT DAY THIRTY

"Last day," I gleefully tell the technician. She's startled and looks at my chart.

"No," she says. "You're scheduled for thirty-three treatments."

"What's happened? They told me only thirty treatments when I started."

She reexamines the chart. "No, thirty-three treatments," she insists. "Do you want to see the chart?" She hands me the chart, a thick document enclosed in ugly brown plastic covers.

I realize that her offer is a professional courtesy. Patients are not ordinarily given their charts to review, and I know that I should take advantage of this unusual opportunity. There was a time when a few sheets of white paper would have been adequate to cover my case. Not now. Over the years the charts have grown thicker and thicker. Everyone puts something in—the nurse, the doctor, the consultants, the pharmacist, the laboratory, the social worker, the intern, the resident, the X-ray department, the clinical psychologist, even the business office. Now records are so thick that no one has time to read them.

I glance at my own chart with distaste and gingerly hand it back to the technician without reading it. I know what doctors write on charts. They describe the patients in unflattering terms. Am I an elderly bald physician who looks older than stated age? Or am I a slightly senile Caucasian? Or an obese elderly male? I could stand that,

I suppose, but on the chart, doctors also write their honest opinion of the illness and the prognosis. That opinion is later matched against the doctor's final examination—the autopsy. Whoever guesses correctly most often wins the prize, best doctor of the year award.

I am terrified at the thought of examining my own chart for fear that someone has recorded in it a poor prognosis. I know that's illogical and that I should look to see if there's an error that could be corrected. But I am no longer able to function as my own doctor. My confidence has been worn down—by my fears about my illness, of course, but also by something more subtle, something that's happened psychologically over these past months.

After the treatment, I ask the doctor, "Why three extra treatments?"

He glances at the chart but doesn't open it, so I suspect it's primarily to be sure that he has my name right. He says, "After we took your X rays and measurements, we put the data in the computer. The answer came out thirty-three treatments. I guess no one told you the results."

The reply shakes me. I have given little thought to how my personal X-ray dosage was determined. In my practice, I gave pills or injections and determined dosage based on age, sex, weight, response, and side effects; it was a relatively simple matter for me to rapidly calculate the individual dosages in my mind. An X-ray dose is much more complicated; there are more variables and less margin for error.

I know of a serious failure in calculation recently in a machine in another hospital that had been miscalibrated by the physicist who installed it. The calibration error went undetected for four years; 592 patients received 14 percent more radiation therapy than their physicians had prescribed.

A team of physicians was sent to investigate the problem. The chief physician told the newspaper reporters that for some patients the excessive dosage might even be a benefit because it takes large doses of X ray to destroy cancer. A year ago, I would have applauded him as being an excellent spokesman, a defender of the faith, but now his response angers me. Did he think that the rest of us are fools?

Computers are used in medicine to control medical devices and machines, but computers and software are man-made and programmed by humans. I knew there had been instances of patients being jeopardized by computer errors, and I knew that the frequency of these errors was increasing as more machinery was introduced into medicine.

A machine similar to the one being used on me killed a thirty-three-year-old man. The man lay on a table beneath the linear accelerator radiation machine. He was at ease. He had already received eight treatments and knew that they were short and painless. But this time, the patient saw a bright flash of light, heard a frying sound, and felt an electrical shock pain in his left shoulder. There were two more bursts. The patient died after being confined to his bed for five months. The machine had malfunctioned due to a computer error, and an X-ray dose many times normal had "zapped" the poor man. This case was not isolated. There had been at least two other deaths associated with that same machine.

I leave the doctor's office, unsatisfied by his explanation of the three "extra" treatments I must take. How could they have failed to tell me of the change? What if I had planned a celebration or a vacation the day my treatment ended? To them, it's all routine. It happens every day. To me, it is very personal—it's my life.

I again begin to feel sorry for myself. I have tried to avoid asking "Why me?" but I was taught by my family that I have a right to my questions, whatever they are.

My grandfather was a religious man. He prayed twice a day, he said numerous blessings over every human function, and he honored the Sabbath and all the holidays. On the days of rest he assiduously studied the Bible.

When I was a boy, I came home from school one day and said, "Zaida, today I learned that the Bible is wrong, that the world was not created in seven days but evolved over millions of years."

And my grandfather said, "The Bible is never wrong. You may have learned a truth, but all the paths of truth eventually meet."

"Does that mean that I should pay no attention to what they teach in school?"

"No," Zaida said, "pay even more attention to what your teachers say, for our sages have commanded us to pursue knowledge and truth wherever those paths may lead."

A week later I fell from my bicycle and split my lip. I bled and I cried, and I said to my mother, "I shouldn't cry because boys don't cry."

She answered, "Boys can cry, but not out loud."

"Was I punished?" I asked. "Because I questioned the Bible?"

"No," she answered. "Questions are never wrong. You were punished because you rode on the streetcar tracks where you don't belong."

Once, when one of my patients in the hospital moaned, "Why me? Why did God do this to me?" her roommate responded, "Why not you? Should it have been me?" I find, however, that when I watch television or listen to the radio, even though I know better, I'm like other humans, and I ask myself, "Why can't I talk like that? Why are their voices so clear and mine so raspy?"

From the beginning of time theologians have been wrestling with the question "Why me?" When I think of all my patients who have been afflicted, I know it is arrogant of me to ask "Why me?" Once I said to a patient, "I'm not God," but I really didn't believe that. If I did, how could I have delegated to myself immortality? How could I have thought, "It won't happen to me"?

To me, illness is not something that people deserve. It is not part of an orderly process that follows rules. Instead, it appears to be a matter of random choice, a matter of luck, like losing in a lottery instead of winning. How else to account for the unfairness of it all?

The most unfair thing of all is the suffering of young people. I have done my best to avoid treating children because I cannot handle death in the young. But sometimes I have gotten stuck. Larry Larson was the all-American teenager. He had the fresh looks of a blue-eyed blond Scandinavian, he grew straight and tall, married his college sweetheart, and got a job with a growing corporation. The happy couple had two boys.

Tragedy struck when Larry was twenty-eight. At first it seemed to be just swollen glands, but when we removed the gland, we knew that Larry had Hodgkin's disease. In those days there were no cancer specialists, so it was up to me to treat him. The prescribed treatment at that time was nitrogen mustard, a gas first used in World War I. Years later, during World War II, a ship carrying nitrogen mustard was sunk in Naples harbor. The dock workers who handled the escaping gases were later found to have lost the white blood cells in their blood. Thus it was decided to use the gas to treat Hodgkin's disease, in which there is a disorder of the white blood cells.

I gave Larry frequent injections of liquid nitrogen mustard, and after each injection, he was sick, sick, sick. I think the treatment was worse than the disease, but what doctor would dare to withhold it when it was the only thing we had to fight off his death?

After two years of suffering, Larry died. If he had lived for a few more years, we could have saved him because a better treatment was developed. He left two small sons, a wife, and his father, Dan. Larry had been an only child, and Dan's salvation was the boys. He became their father and companion, going with them fishing, camping, and to Little League.

I lost track of the family, and I understood what had

happened. Why should they see me? I reminded them of their tragedy. I was a loser.

Ten years after his son's death, Dan came to my office with one of his grandsons, the eldest. Now eighteen, the boy was the image of his father, blond, straight, stalwart, and handsome. He was a promising baseball pitcher, but recently he had seemed to be losing control of his right arm.

Grandpa suspected what was wrong and I had to confirm his suspicions. His grandson, his life and his salvation, had Lou Gehrig's disease, or amyotrophic lateral sclerosis. Like his father before him, the son was doomed; and I once more had to bear the sad tidings.

Life is not fair. I, a doctor, of all people, should know that. What right do I have to ask for an exception for myself?

TREATMENT DAY THIRTY-ONE

Today the receptionist greets me with, "Good morning, Mr. Rosenbaum."

Five weeks of treatment, and I am no longer a doctor. A few months ago I was a captain, a man of position and power; then she would have been properly respectful. Now I am just a patient. Soon she will be calling me Ed. With a start, I say to myself, "I've done the same." In the medical profession we often call patients by their first names. We remain "Doctor" or "Nurse," while they lose their titles and respect. How often have I done that to the people I have treated? Too often.

Usually a technician conducts me to a treatment room. Today the secretary motions for me to follow her, explaining, "The therapists are busy, so I'll put you in your room."

I am left standing in a room that is bare except for the treatment table. I can hear the technicians quarreling in the hallway.

Sweet, friendly Debbie says, "You treat him today. It's time for my coffee break."

They are talking about me!

Barbara answers, "No way! I'm too busy."

I've always thought I was special to Barbara. I never once stopped to think that she treats thirty patients a day. What difference is there between one patient and the other? It's a routine, dull job.

Debbie seems angry. "I'm entitled to my break. I'll let him wait."

"Better not," Barbara warns. "We're booked solid. We'll fall behind schedule."

"Okay," Debbie says, "but I'm not going to miss my coffee break. I'll turn him over to the students."

Two students enter the room, unaware that I have heard the entire conversation in the hallway. They are so green, they can't even find the tattoo marks on my neck. I'm in a state of shock. They'll never center the machine properly! I'm also furious with Debbie and Barbara: this is much too crucial a procedure to leave to students. If the X-ray beam is off, the treatment is useless and I could be burned. It's like having an intern do surgery on me to gain experience. I am resentful that I'm the one they are practicing on.

I direct the students. "Use the size D head block. Don't forget the supports under my knees."

I have already had thirty treatments. Always they have started on the right side first. Now the student starts on the left. I hear her say under her breath, "The machine is already on the left side, so let's start there and save the trouble of moving it." The substitute concurs. Ra-

tionally, I am pretty sure that it doesn't make any difference what side they begin on, but I am on edge. Any
change upsets me. I listen as the cassette that determines
the site of the treatment area is clicked into place. The
click just doesn't sound right; it doesn't sound the same
as when the regular technician is working.

Now comes the call, "Lights on." Both technicians
scurry out of the room to avoid any X-ray exposure to
themselves. Then the lights go off again, and a whirring
sound begins, the sound of the X rays being generated.
I begin to count. I know the time, thirty seconds on each
side. If it runs thirty-one seconds, I am determined that
I am going to jump off the table. How can I be certain
that these beginners can set the machine?

In thirty seconds the sound clicks off. The left side is
now done, and the treatment seems to proceed as usual,
though I am rigid with tension, counting the interminable
thirty seconds for the other side.

The lights come back on. "Let go of the ropes," they
tell me now, "the treatment's over." The machine rotates over my head again. The table is lowered, and I sit
up to sounds of laughter and chatter. Now there are three
technicians in the room, the two beginners and Debbie.

"What's so funny?" I demand. "Where have you
been, Debbie?"

"Having a late breakfast," she says calmly. "The unit
secretary brought in my favorite bagels, cream cheese,
and lox. I can't resist that."

I am angry, but what right have I to object? I have
taught students all my professional life. I have been an
advocate of the student learning by doing. I can't begin
to count the number of student procedures that I have
supervised—but up until now, the procedures have been
on other people, not on me. On patients.

One of the penalties of being treated in medical schools
is that students do learn on the patients. A recent study
has shown that a doctor does not perfect his skill with a
procedure until he has done that procedure more than a

hundred times. I can only hope that I was at least the ninety-ninth patient for these radiology students.

TREATMENT DAY THIRTY-TWO

The extra treatment days mean that the last treatment days come on Rosh Hashanah, one of the holiest days of the Jewish religion, the day of meditation, the day for settling of all debts between man and man, and man and God.

In all my years I have always gone to the synagogue on Rosh Hashanah and Yom Kippur. A time of crisis is not exactly a time to skip the synagogue, but the decision for me is obvious. As I understand it, Judaism teaches that life is precious and health takes precedence over religion. If it's a question of health or ritual, ritual must give way. And yet the decision isn't always clear-cut.

Many years ago, a very well-dressed elderly woman, Marion Bronstein, was brought to the hospital with a hip fracture. A young Jewish doctor was in the emergency room, and he operated on her hip immediately.

As he came out of the anesthetic, the patient held on to the doctor's hands and lamented, "Doctor, we have sinned. Today is Yom Kippur, a day we are forbidden to work, when we should be concentrating on prayer and meditation. You have sinned, because you have worked. I have sinned, because I caused you to work."

The doctor was a fast thinker. "Don't worry, Mrs. Bronstein," he assured her, "before I operated on you I called the rabbi and he gave me permission to go ahead, so it's all right.''

The incident set the physician thinking: he hadn't been to the synagogue in years. When he left the hospital, he went to the temple, sat in a pew, and listened to the cantor chant the ancient Hebrew words. By the time the service was over, he had made a decision.

On hospital rounds the next day, he examined Mrs. Bronstein and told her, "Listen. I've figured it out. If I charge for yesterday's operation, it will be a sin because it will be counted as work and I'll get a black mark beside my name in the eternal book. So the surgery's free, a gift. Happy New Year!"

"Never!" the elderly woman said firmly. "Then the sin will be on me."

The story was in my mind when I checked in for the treatment on Rosh Hashanah, so I said to the secretary, "Today ought to be a free treatment day."

"Why?" she asked.

"Because it's Rosh Hashanah."

"Don't worry," she said, "we'll bill Medicare."

TREATMENT DAY THIRTY-THREE

This really is the last day, and the technician tells me that the doctor wants to see me before the treatment.

"What's wrong?"

"Nothing. It's routine. He always sees his patients on their last day."

As I wait in a consultation room, Mrs. Duggin walks

by. It's been over two weeks since I have seen her, and she is clearly failing. I'm afraid she isn't going to make it, and I don't really want to talk to her. I have all I can do to handle my own problems. I don't have any energy left for anyone else.

But Mrs. Duggin sees me and enters the room smiling. "Congratulations," she says. "You've finished the course."

"How much longer do you have?" I ask.

"Two more weeks."

I hurt for her. When I was in practice, I would have known how to offer her some consolation, but now I am too entwined in my own problem. I know that I have a chance; we both know her time is short. Then Mrs. Duggin does something that demonstrates that we belong to the same exclusive club. We share secrets no one else can. In that cramped little room, she takes off the scarf and reveals to me her bare skull with its two-inch square tattoo.

But I don't see a bald woman. I see only the beautiful smiling face of a madonna. My impatient self-involvement has vanished. I say what is in my heart: "I know the doctors are wrong."

She only nods before she leaves the room, but her strength and courage have done more for my spirit than any of my doctors have accomplished. How I wish I could help her!

The technician returns. "The doctor can't see you. He's been called out."

"What now?"

"You're to get your treatment, and his assistant will see you."

I angrily blurt out, "Half the time I don't see my doctor. It's my last day, for God's sake. I don't want to be seen by asistants, residents, and interns. I want to see my own physician."

"Don't worry. Dr. Blum is as good as Dr. Reed."

I take my treatment and go back to the examining

room. Dr. Blum is older than I expect him to be, and he says very little. Radiologists are not very communicative. He proceeds with the fiberoptic examination. He pushes the scope through my nose, and, unlike the others, he doesn't even bother with a local anesthetic. I am surprised that I have such little distress. He appears to be competent with the instrument. He takes his time with the examination. When he finally removes the scope, there is a smile on his face. He is the first physician who has smiled at me in two months. "Looks good," he says.

That sounds good, but I go home unsatisfied. His optimism is, I know, premature. It is too early to know whether the treatment has been successful. Dr. Blum has forgotten that I am a doctor; he is treating me like a patient, offering me offhand, easy assurance. Well, would I rather he just said, "We can't be sure yet"? Yes, I would. I don't want false-positive reports.

Phil was one of my best friends. He returned from a hunting trip complaining of a cough and a cold. He didn't have a cold, he had lung cancer. The Xrays showed it, and a biopsy of the glands in his neck proved it. But I did not believe it.

I sent him to an oncologist, who started drug therapy. Phil hated it. He would start to vomit when he got in his car to drive to the treatment. I dreaded visiting him in the hospital. He had been a rugged man, handsome and successful. Now he had the drawn, sallow look of a failing cancer patient. His thick head of black hair was gone, his eyes were sunken, and no matter how much sedation he got, he would vomit and vomit.

When chemotherapy was first introduced, because of its terrible side effects, I advised my patients to forget it and to die in peace. But as the years went on, I saw that some patients who had the treatment recovered. How could I possibly advise my friend Phil not to try it? I had no way to predict the outcome.

One evening, after three months of suffering, Phil and

his wife came to our house bearing bottles of champagne. They were overjoyed. The oncologist had just told them that the chest X ray showed no evidence of the lesion. The cancer had disappeared.

I knew better. I knew that the X ray could not detect the microscopic cancer cells that were lurking in the lungs. It would be only a matter of months before there would be a recurrence. But I held my words and choked on the champagne while Phil and his wife lived in a fool's paradise. Six months later, it was all over.

I wanted to believe Dr. Blum's reassuring words about my own situation, but I couldn't be sure that I wasn't getting the same treatment that my friend had received.

THE AFTERMATH

ONE WEEK POSTTREATMENT

It is the day after Yom Kippur. I didn't like the rabbi's sermon yesterday. He spoke of the Biblical allowance of years, three score and ten. Everything else is a bonus. On Yom Kippur the books are closed, and then it is inscribed who shall live and who shall die, who shall fail and who shall prosper.

Dee awakens me. "What do you want to do today?" she asks. I look out. It's gloomy and raining.

"Nothing."

"What did you say?"

"Nothing," I repeat.

"Say that again!"

"Can't you hear?" I snap.

"Say it again and again," she laughs. "Your voice is back!"

I repeat the words and listen to myself. She's right. For the first time in months, my voice sounds almost normal.

"I have been inscribed for another year in the Book of Life," I tell Dee.

It is still cloudy and raining, but I now see that autumn is a time not of death but of harvest and rejoicing. The Oregon rain after a dry summer is liquid sunshine. It promises rejuvenation and a renewal of life.

TEN DAYS POSTTREATMENT

Ten days ago I thought I had recovered, that the ordeal was over, but when I look in the mirror this morning my face is distorted and my left eye swollen shut. I am very frightened.

"It's only an insect bite," I tell Dee.

But every few minutes I examine my face in the mirror. By late morning, small blisters have developed. By late afternoon, I have pain and more swelling. I've never seen a bite like this.

Then I say to myself, "Stop being stupid. You delayed going to a doctor in the first place and got into trouble. Don't do it again. Call."

First I call the medical school, but my physicians are gone for the day: Thursday, golf day. Only the residents are available, but I don't want to be seen by a beginner.

Then I call Aaron Dome, a friend and dermatologist. I tell him the truth. I explain that the swelling started in the morning, I called my doctors, they were not available, and I delayed calling him until late afternoon.

I used to get angry when patients did that. I'd say, "They get sick in the morning, they can't reach their own doctor, then they wait till night to call me."

But Aaron is cordial, maybe because of the many patients I've referred to him. He politely says, "We're all done for the day, but I'll wait for you in the office. Come right over."

After he examines my skin, he says, "I'm not sure. To

152

me it looks like a strep infection—old-fashioned erysip-elas. I'll have my partner take a look."

The opinion alarms me. Before antibiotics were available, erysipelas, a streptococcal skin infection, was common, and it could be fatal. As a senior medical student I assisted at an autopsy on a patient who died from erysipelas. The infection had started over the left eye, just like mine.

Aaron's partner's opinion is bad. "Could be a lym-phoma or a viral infection."

Both suggest a punch biopsy of the skin. I don't want to have my face cut. I wonder why they are in such a hurry to operate. I know that if we wait a couple of days, the diagnosis will become evident, but the suggestion that it might be a lymphoma worries me; so I permit the proce-dure.

After the biopsy is done, we have a three-way consul-tation. As so often happens in medicine, we are three doc-tors with three different opinions. Aaron says, "I think it's a strep infection. We won't know for twenty-four hours, but if it is strep, it could be fatal in twenty-four hours. Start penicillin."

Aaron's partner says, "I don't think it's strep, I think it's viral. We don't have a treatment for viruses, but start Zovirax. It's a new antiviral agent. Who knows? It might work."

If we don't know what the diagnosis is, and if we don't know if the medicine will work, it doesn't make sense to take anything. But like most patients and most doctors, I feel the need to do something. So, illogical as it is, I agree to take another course of penicillin.

The next morning I am no better. Dee insists on another consultation. I call Dr. Reed's office, but he is in Miami delivering a paper. I think, I have the greatest doctor in the world, but what good is he to me if he's in Miami? This is the fourth time I've been unable to see him.

Reluctantly I consent to see his associate. It is a busy morning in the X-ray department. The associate is over-loaded with patients. He takes a quick glance at my swollen eye and says, "It doesn't belong in our department. It's not from X ray, see the dermatologists." That's what doctors always do when they don't know or don't want to be bothered.

In the evening my son Jim, the immunologist, sees me. "Dad," he says, "it's shingles—herpes zoster, a complication of X-ray therapy. I've seen cases like it when I was at Stanford."

I now know how some of my patients felt when I referred them to another doctor for a second opinion and the opinion was different. Now I, too, have to wrestle with several opinions. I, too, don't know which one is correct.

Here's the score so far:

Dermatologist 1: It's erysipelas.

Dermatologist 2: It's a virus, maybe a lymphoma.

Radiologist: I don't know. It's not due to Xray therapy, and it doesn't belong in my department.

My son Jim: It's shingles.

Myself: I hope it's an insect bite, but it must be a lymphoma.

It's just happened to my neighbor, Arnie James. When he injured his back, his doctor, a general practitioner, said, "Lumbosacral sprain." When he didn't improve, Arnie consulted an orthopedist, who said, "Spondylolisthesis [slipped vertebra]." Next, a psychiatrist said, "No physical disease, a mental state—a clear case of compensation neurosis."

After three months of persistent back pain, Arnie came to me, a rheumatologist. "The previous doctors were wrong." I said, "You're in the early stages of ankylosing spondylitis [arthritis of the spine]."

"Oh, no," another rheumatologist said, "the X rays and the laboratory tests are normal. He has fibrositis [muscular rheumatism]."

A neurosurgeon was brought in. His verdict? "They are all wrong. He has a disk, slipped cartilage. He needs surgery."

A second neurosurgeon was brought in. His verdict? "He doesn't need surgery. I can inject an enzyme that will dissolve the disk cartilage."

"Don't do it," a neurologist told the bewildered patient. "You'll get well with time."

Every doctor who treats chronic back problems has had similar situations. Arnie hurt my feelings; even though I was his neighbor, he finally placed himself under the care of a chiropractor. I haven't examined him in years, but he looks okay to me.

After forty-eight hours of suspense, my biopsy proves that I have shingles. I have mixed emotions about that report. I take pride in the fact that my son was right, but am I being replaced by my son as king of the hill, or was my judgment impaired by my being the patient? The thing that really bothers me is that once again I made a bad choice. If I had listened to the second doctor and taken Zovirax instead of the penicillin, I might have aborted the shingles.

Shingles mean that my resistance is down. The white blood cells of the body are charged with the duty to defend a person against all invaders. There are different types of white cells, each with different functions, but they act in unison. When an invader such as a bacterium, a virus, a fungus, a protozoan, or a cancer cell attacks, an alarm is sounded and the white cells respond. The invader is repelled, and its profile is forever recorded so that if it reappears, the body can respond promptly.

These cells, acting in unison, are known as the immune system. This system can be impaired by nutrition, age, drugs, X rays, fatigue, and emotions. In AIDS, the immune system is impaired because a virus has sneaked into the body undetected and has attached itself to some of the white cells, destroying their ability to function. When the immune system does not function properly, a person is liable to develop cancer or to become a victim of an infection which ordinarily would not cause any illness.

Shingles is an adult form of chicken pox, a disease so highly contagious that in our urban society few children escape it. When a child has chicken pox and recovers, the virus is not destroyed; it remains in the body in a dormant state, doing no harm. Later in life, if an adult who has had chicken pox develops an impairment of the immune system, the virus may become active again and cause a new illness, shingles. In the adult, the virus attacks the nervous system and manifests itself by redness, blisters, and pain along a nerve pathway. There is no specific treatment, but the disease is seldom fatal and with time most patients recover completely. In rare cases the immune system may be so suppressed that the disease becomes generalized, and then it is fatal. I have seen hundreds of cases of shingles in my lifetime; all but one of the patients recovered without incident, but that one patient died. Now that I have the disease, I can think only of her.

She was a young woman with breast cancer. During her operation she was found to have cancer in one lymph node. Because of this, she was given a course of chemotherapy. Unfortunately, the chemotherapy so suppressed her immune system that she developed shingles, which became generalized and resulted in death. She died of her treatment, not from her disease. Today, maybe Zovirax would have saved her.

I too am a victim of iatrogenic disease, a disease caused by medical treatment: My X-ray treatment caused my shingles. The ancient dictum to physicians, "Do no harm," was so easy to follow in the early days of my practice. Most medical therapy was relatively innocuous, and side effects were rare. As therapy improved, the risks of adverse effects increased. It's so easy to say to the patient that we must weigh the benefits against the risks, and then add that the risks are infinitesimal. Even when the risks are one in a thousand, for the one unlucky patient who develops a side effect, the risk is too high.

Ten percent of all patients admitted to a hospital are there because of iatrogenic disease. Usually the side effects are statistically predictable. I can say to a patient that there is one chance in a hundred that he or she will react unfavorably to a treatment, but I cannot select that one patient. Sometimes the side effects are new and have never been seen by doctors before, as happened when thalidomide was given to expectant mothers and they bore children with serious birth defects.

Thirty years ago, chloroquine, an antimalarial drug, was used as a treatment for rheumatoid arthritis. I gave it to a ten-year-old girl, and a few months later her mother called me in tears: "Not only is my daughter crippled with arthritis, but she is aging. Her hair is turning gray." Sure enough, when I examined her, her red hair was streaked with gray. Subsequently, it was learned that chloroquine could cause graying of the hair, but only in redheads. Up until that time, no such side effect had been known. Fortunately, it was reversible.

Now I am a victim of iatrogenic disease. True, I would have taken the X-ray therapy even if it could have been predicted that I would develop shingles. But now that I have shingles, even though it was only a one-in-a-thousand chance, I am worried because it means that my immune system is compromised. If I survive this disease, my chances of developing another form of cancer are greater than the average. But some victims of iatrogenic disease are not so lucky, sometimes they become gravely ill. Sometimes they die.

FIVE WEEKS POSTTREATMENT

Today I am to see Dr. DuVall, who will determine whether the therapy has been effective. Today is the day of truth. Dr. DuVall was the doctor who made the diagnosis, performed the biopsy, and recommended the therapy. He has not seen me since I began the X-ray treatment.

I am tired; I have had a restless night. I have had dreams about my childhood, about my grandparents and parents, very similar to the dreams that I had before the operation.

I anticipate the worst scenario, and I wonder what words the doctor will use to convey the bad news. Will he be blunt and say, "You're incurable" or "The treatment has failed"? Or will he use such terms as "You're in relative remission"? or "You're in partial remission"? In all my years of experience, I have never been able to find the right phrase. I have tried "Have you thought about the future?" or "I would like to talk to your family." I've tried them all, but nothing seems right. No wonder.

The wait to see the doctor is not unreasonable—ten minutes in the reception room and then ten minutes in the examining room—but it seems like hours. As soon as the doctor comes in, I watch his face for an expression, though that doesn't make sense for he hasn't even examined me. There are the usual greetings and questions. My answers are brief. I don't want to socialize; I want the doctor to hurry and complete the examination.

He anesthetizes my throat and then leaves the room, for it will be at least five minutes before the anesthetic takes effect. It's a normal way to act, but it no longer seems that way to me. I don't want to be left alone at this time. Why doesn't he understand that?

That's the way doctors are. When they start as medical students, they lavish time and empathy on their first patients. By the time they have finished their training, they have seen thousands of patients, and the process has become routine. By the time they are in practice, seeing twenty or thirty patients a day, they have learned not to get too involved. In the past, when they got too involved, they were badly bruised if the patient died. Now that I've had this experience, I'll try to do better when I return to my practice. But if I develop empathy, will my decisions be rational? Will I myself be overwhelmed by my more personal involvement?

When Dr. DuVall returns and passes the scope, I watch his face as he has me say, "Aaaaaaah, eeeeeeee." He carefully removes the scope, and I can sense from his smile that everything is okay so far.

I want him to tell me that I'm cured, but he doesn't do that. He says only, "So far, so good," and then adds, "I will repeat this examination once a month for two years and then once every three months for life. I will know your larynx like the palm of my hand."

In half an hour this morning, I have learned more about handling the seriously ill patient than in fifty years of practice. I must tell my colleagues about this. These are the things we must do:

First, no waiting. We must solve this problem of waiting. To us the visits are routine, to the patients the waiting is torture. It makes them suffer or it makes them very hostile, even before they get to see you.

If you have bad news, spit it out. Do it kindly, but don't delay or embellish the truth so much that it makes the situation worse.

Don't be afraid to express your emotions. Show your sympathy on your face and say it with words.

Be gentle in all procedures. If you can't learn to do it properly, have someone else do it.

As I leave his office, I turn to Dr. DuVall and thank him. And as I drive home, I realize how many patients say thank you, even when the doctor has goofed or told them bad news. On the other hand, patients whom I have helped sometimes have been the least thankful. Perhaps that's because the diagnosis was quick, the treatment was successful, and they never had a chance to appreciate the skill and effort that went into their care. Ironically, in cases where the diagnosis has been delayed, where the tests have been endless, where there has been pain and anxiety, the patients have understood and appreciated the effort.

Even when they are given bad news, patients often thank the physician because they are anxious to please him or her, and the doctor is so flattered, he doesn't realize that he may have failed to help. This happened once when I asked an orthopedic surgeon to operate on a patient's arthritic knee. The doctor was so delighted with the results that he presented her case to the medical staff as a new, successful surgical approach for the arthritic knee. When I pointed out that the patient was still in bed, still unable to walk, and still in pain, the surgeon got very angry with me. I asked him to visit the patient so as to demonstrate to him that he was a victim of wishful thinking. But when he got to her home, the woman was so flattered that even though she wasn't any better, she blessed him and thanked him for coming.

It's not so funny. I've just thanked my own doctor. What for? I'm sick. I'm still not cured.

BITTER MEDICINE

Now I taste a new and bitter pill—medical bills. Since starting medical school, I have never received a doctor's bill. Any care we needed was provided as a matter of professional courtesy.

In World War II, when I was with the Army Medical Corps in North Africa, a doctor in our outfit received a letter from his wife in Chicago; she'd needed medical care and the doctor she'd seen had sent a bill. The medical officers were incensed. Here we were, risking our lives, and this colleague at home had the gall to break the unwritten gentleman's code. Who had ever heard of one doctor billing another? What was the world coming to? No doubt about it, the good men had gone to war and the country was deteriorating. We sent a letter to the American Medical Association asking them to straighten out this erring colleague.

Naturally, when I was in private practice, I used to send patients bills, but like most doctors, I insulated myself from the actual process. Billing was the job of clerks and bookkeepers. Now that I receive bills, I understand the patient's frustration with the process. The amount I owe stuns me: a thousand dollars for a day's hospitalization! Even though I am a doctor, I cannot understand the itemized charges in the hospital bill. Some charges are labeled miscellaneous. What is that? There are charges for drugs I never heard of, and there are ridiculous charges for inexpensive items such as tissues and aspirin.

Medicare was introduced to help senior citizens, yet

to fill out a Medicare form is worse than filling out a tax return. I can't understand the way Medicare's billing process is computerized and coded. One day it pays for an X ray, the next day it refuses to pay for the same X ray; it all depends on which operator puts the data into the computer. Something like that happened to my eighty-year-old aunt, Thia Crout, who insisted that she had unusual fatigue that could only be helped by monthly injections of vitamin B_{12}. When she wintered in Palm Springs, California, a doctor there gave her these injections and Medicare paid for them. When she returned to Portland and I gave her the vitamin injections, Medicare refused to pay for them. I wrote a letter saying, "Dear Sirs: I know that vitamin B_{12} does not help fatigue. You know that vitamin B_{12} does not help fatigue. The problem is that my aunt, Mrs. Crout, does not know that vitamin B_{12} does not help fatigue. She also does not understand why it works in California and not in Oregon, since you pay for it in California and not in Oregon. Will you please write and explain the matter to her."

Shortly thereafter I received a call from Medicare's local medical adviser. I thought he was a friend of mine until he said, "Why don't you go to hell, Ed?" And he refused to write to my Aunt Thia.

Recognizing how complicated the problem of billing is, we have trained clerks in our office who do all the insurance forms and billing for our patients. If I had a doctor so haughty that he refused to give me any help with these matters, I would change doctors.

It's not only the matter of money that disturbs me. I sense that during the past nine months of my illness I have been undergoing a metamorphosis. What has happened to me? To my mind, I have been privileged to belong to an honored profession dedicated to the welfare of mankind. In the past years I have been a spokesman for my colleagues and a defender of my profession. My position has been steadfast: We are an honorable fraternity dedicated to the welfare of mankind.

In 1962, representing the American Medical Association and speaking before a congressional committee, I said, "I challenge anyone to produce any resident of Oregon who has been denied medical care because of need." The challenge was never met.

I offered this guarantee: "Doctors of Oregon will accept the responsibility and see to it that every citizen in this state receives medical care, regardless of ability to pay."

Now the old days are gone. For the most part, those I spoke for are retired or dead. A new generation is in charge, and they have not authorized me to speak for them. Even if they asked, I couldn't, for I can no longer hurl the challenge or offer the guarantee.

Medicine has changed. We used to be a calling that catered to the public welfare, and our prime consideration was the patient. Now we are a business, and some of us practice as impersonal corporations, with the bottom line the profits, not the well-being of the patient.

Like big business, we advertise, and our ads are self-serving and superficial. In spite of what the ads promise, a mammogram does not always detect early breast cancer; the hospitals' new Alzheimer's clinics can offer little help, as we have no treatment for Alzheimer's disease; the ads do not truthfully tell the patients who best can treat alcoholism, drug addiction, or depression; and doctors do take postgraduate courses, but instead of studying the latest scientific advances, the courses are on office management, billing, and public relations.

A Harvard Medical School professor, in a published article, has stated that prior to 1911, the average patient who saw a doctor was worse off than the patient who didn't. That is to say, a sick person who stayed away from doctors had a better chance of recovery than the patient who went for medical care. (We have seen much more recent studies that show that during periods when few doctors have been available, death rates have declined)

* * *

I graduated from medical school in 1938. Even in those days, medicine was more a priesthood than a science. A favorite examination question was, ''If you are lost on a desert island with only six drugs, which drugs would suffice for good medical practice?'' The answer was arsenicals for syphilis, quinine for malaria, insulin for diabetes, liver for pernicious anemia, digitalis for the heart, and morphine for pain. All other medicines were pure placebo, worthless except for their psychological value. Surgery was largely limited to bone setting, tonsillectomies, and the removal of organs in the abdomen. The obstetricians knew that the less they did, the better the patient did. They were admonished by their teachers, ''Wait, don't interfere, let nature do the delivery.''

Modern medicine started with the discovery of antibiotics, but there are still infections we can't cure; for instance, we have no good treatment for virus infections. Our treatment for many strokes, multiple sclerosis, and Alzheimer's disease is possibly a notch above placebo therapy.

And our increasing intervention with high-tech medicine and surgical procedures has been a mixed blessing.

We have removed tonsils, adenoids and uteruses that should never have been removed and have often justified it by saying that they were foci of infection.

We have treated enlarged thymus glands in children with Xray therapy on the questionable theory that an enlarged gland was harmful. Later in life, because of our Xray treatment, the thymus became cancerous.

We have given mothers DES to prevent miscarriages, and as a result their daughters subsequently developed cancer of the genital tract.

We have given pregnant women thalidomide to help them sleep, and due to the drug their children were born deformed.

We have given appetite suppressants to help patients lose weight, and they became blind because the drug induced cataracts.

The list seems endless. Unwittingly we have given drugs

that have killed instead of cured and performed surgeries on patients that have maimed instead of helped.

I have known doctors and even spokesmen for the cancer societies who, when they themselves developed cancer, have abandoned conventional medicine for unconventional therapy. They know what a layperson usually does not; taken as a whole, the cure rate for cancer is only 60 percent.

The irony of medicine is that doctors are honored and respected for being devoted to helping the sick, yet they make their money from the patient's misery. Thus far, no one has solved the problem of separating medicine from economics. Even turning the matter over to the state has not solved the problem, for then it becomes a matter of politicians and taxes.

I knew a priest once who came up with a partial solution for one of his parishioners. The patient was in the prime of life, a forty-five-year-old executive with a wife and two small children. He had been involved in a head-on collision and was comatose for weeks. It became apparent that he was not going to recover. The problem is common now, but at that time we still had not developed today's sophisticated methods to keep a hopelessly comatose patient alive. Still, we were beginning to make inroads in maintaining a semblance of life in such patients. This man was under thermal blankets for temperature control, he was on a respirator for breathing, he was given intravenous fluids for food and water. And so he continued to live in his unconscious vegetable state. It had gone on for some months when his wife protested to the doctors and to the hospital that their medical insurance policy was exhausted. She had no other resources, and she knew that she would be left a penniless widow. No one was able to help. The doctors and the hospital advised her that ethics demanded that they exert every effort to keep the hopeless patient alive. I was unable to offer a solution.

The woman consulted her parish priest, who called the hospital administrator and explained the situation to him

thus: ''In one week the family's medical insurance policy
will be exhausted. This woman has no personal funds, and
she now has to support herself. I have advised her that she
has no moral obligation to pay the doctor and the hospital
bills once the insurance policy is gone.''

Somehow or other, within a matter of a few days, both
the doctor and the hospital found a reason to stop the ox-
ygen, the thermal blankets, the intravenous fluids, and the
constant nursing attention. The patient was transferred to
a nursing home. (In spite of the lack of supporting care,
as sometimes happens, he continued to live for five more
years.)

I don't want to overreact. In spite of its failure, medicine has had its successes. In my lifetime we have controlled diabetes, pernicious anemia, high blood pressure,
and many infectious diseases. We are able to operate with
some success on the heart, the lungs, and the brain. We
are able to replace diseased joins with artificial joints that
work. Even some forms of cancer are now being cured,
and other types are being slowed down. I find myself having to stress these positive things to hold on to my faith.

BACK AT WORK

OCTOBER—FIRST DAY

A s my illness has progressed, and as it has forced me to think about my profession, I have vowed that I would return to work a better, more understanding doctor. On the very first day back, I am put to the test. Before I have time to read my mail, Dr. McDee, the radiologist, pushes into my office.

"I have bad news," he announces.

"Spill it."

"Mrs. Lindblum has a lesion in her esophagus."

"Show me."

I follow him into the X-ray room, and we examine the films.

"I can see it," I say. "Think it's malignant?"

"Yep."

"How do you know?"

"Look at the irregularity."

"Does she have trouble swallowing?"

"Why do you think I ordered the upper GI?"

"Well, you're right; it's malignant."

Because of my recent experience, I know the anxiety Mrs. Lindblum is suffering, and I realize that I have violated my first vow. I have kept her waiting while I reviewed the X-ray films and discussed her problem with the radiologist.

Finally I escort her to the consultation room. I offer her a chair, and I say, "You have a tumor."

"A tumor?" she asks.

"Yes, a growth."

169

"A growth?"

"Yes. It's probably malignant."

She breaks out into a cold sweat. I have never noticed that in patients before, but now I know what to expect. I hand her a paper cup of water.

"What next?" she asks.

"I will have to arrange for a gastroscopic examination. The doctor will pass a flexible scope down your throat, look into your esophagus, and remove a small section of tissue to examine. Not as bad as it sounds. You will be sedated but half awake."

"Is the procedure dangerous?" she asks.

I wonder if I should tell her of the risk of the instrument perforating her esophagus, but I can't. Instead, I risk a malpractice suit, and I reassure her. I say, "No."

It takes an hour before I reach the gastroenterologist to arrange for an examination—five days from now.

When it is all over, I reflect that I haven't handled the patient any better now than I would have done before. I have kept her waiting; I haven't found a way to lessen her anxiety. All I have learned is to have her sitting down when I tell her the diagnosis was cancer.

But today there is something different: my feelings. I feel like I did when I was an intern, and for the first time in my life I had to tell a patient's family that he had cancer. The calluses accumulated over fifty years are suddenly stripped away, my nerves are raw, I feel for Mrs. Lindblum, and I am unable to control my trembling as I tell her the bad news.

OCTOBER—FOURTH WEEK

The first weeks in the office, I work half days because of fatigue. On one busy morning, the receptionist hands me a note. "Dr. Reed's secretary says to call when you're not busy."

"What's her number?"

"She didn't give it to me," my secretary replies. "She said you would know, so I didn't insist."

I am furious. "I don't know a Dr. Reed, so how would I know his number?" I admonish the receptionist. "If someone expects a return call, take his number. Now that you don't have it, look it up."

Later in the morning the secretary tells me, "I can't find his name in the phone book."

"Of course," I respond sarcastically. "He's probably a Ph.D., not an M.D. Look in the white pages."

A few minutes later I am buzzed on the intercom. "I have Dr. Reed's number. He's at the medical school. His secretary's on the line. She wants to change your appointment with him."

"Oh, God," I gasp. "I'm sorry. He's my personal physician. How could I have forgotten his name?"

I am doing what my patients do. I am burying in my subconscious mind something that I want to forget. I am denying my illness. Now that I am back on the job, I want to forget the whole thing.

I remember the lessons I taught medical students. Their first day on the wards, a cluster of medical students would gather around me, eager to put their hands on a live patient.

"Doctors," I addressed them formally. It would be two more years before they would earn their medical degree, but today I wanted them to experience for the first time the responsibilities that accompany the title. "The most important part of the patient examination is the history. It sounds so simple: just ask and you'll be told. But it ain't so. You seldom get a straight answer. Taking a history is not simple. It is an art that will take you a lifetime to learn. You think that people will tell you why they have come to see you, but they don't. They forget, they exaggerate, or they ignore what is important. A good history at this stage of your career will take at least one or two hours. Who would like to be the first to try?"

Al Cann, bubbling, rosy-cheeked, rotund, with all the exuberance of a twenty-three-year-old medical student, volunteered.

"Okay," I instructed him, "let's start with the patient in this room."

The patient was a young man the age of the students. He was sitting expressionlessly on the bed in a hospital robe. Al started the history as he had been taught. Why are you here? How old are you? How long have you had symptoms? Etc., etc., etc.

The patient responded, "I am nervous, my heart pounds, my palms sweat."

Al asked, "Do you have headaches?"

The patient said, "Yes."

"Do you have heartburn?"

"Yes."

"Do you have distress on urination?"

"Yes."

And so it went. To every symptom Al inquired about, the patient responded in the affirmative.

After an hour we retreated to the hallway.

"What do you think?" I asked the students.

They all agreed that the patient was suffering from emotional stress.

"Good," I congratulated them. "Now let's go back and see what I get when I ask the questions."

We reentered the room. "You seem anxious," I said to the patient.

"I am," he said.

"Have you ever seen a psychiatrist for your problems?"

"Yes."

"Who?"

He then named every prominent psychiatrist in the community.

"Why do you think you're nervous?" I asked.

"Because I am bisexual and my marriage is failing."

"Did you ever tell that to the psychiatrists?"

"No."

"Why not?"

"They never asked me," he answered.

Back in the hall we discussed the history.

"You see," I explained to the students, "how stubborn people are and why it takes us over an hour to get simple information?"

I used to wonder, why are people so weak? Why do they persist in burying unpleasant facts in their subconscious mind? Today I discover that I, too, am an ordinary mortal. What I don't like, I forget. I know how to take a history and how to bring patients back to reality. That isn't the problem. The difficulty lies in the fact that I have told stories like this on my patients, making a joke about how limited they are in their understanding. I'm not limited. I know as much as anyone about most aspects of medical diagnoses and treatment. And still I blocked out the name of my own physician. Why? Because he was treating me for cancer. And probably, if he knew what had happened, he'd tell a story on me: "I had this patient who was a well-known physician, and you know what happened when he got sick himself . . . ?''

NOVEMBER—SIXTH WEEK

I have been back in practice six weeks. Events that I used to shrug off now bother me. I know that it relates to my own illness. I take my patients' misfortunes more personally. I find it difficult to convey bad news, and I wonder if this is impairing my function as a physician. I can no longer completely detach myself.

Today Betty died. I know because an emergency room doctor in Palm Springs called to notify me. He didn't know the cause of death, only that she'd had a cardiac arrest. I have cared for Betty since she was a little girl. She had juvenile rheumatoid arthritis. She died in her thirty-fifth year.

What bothers me is, why did she die? Where did I fail? I saw her just two weeks ago and told her she could go away for a vacation. Did she die of an unusual sensitivity to one of the drugs I was giving her? Did she develop a new disease? I certainly would not have predicted her death. I have failed her. I won't know what happened until I receive the autopsy report, and even then we still may not know the cause of her death.

I feel very depressed. I've been at this for so long, yet every time it happens there is the same depression and the same guilt. I am supposed to prevent death. The truth is that I always fail. Sometimes I am lucky and forestall the inevitable, but in the end I always lose. The depression always comes, but it disappears in a few days because I cannot allow it to take over; I must go on.

Now it's worse than ever.

I know Betty's relatives. They regard me as part of their family. I will have to go to the funeral, and I dread that. At times like these I have a fantasy. I am convinced that everyone at the funeral will be pointing at me and saying, "That's her doctor who goofed." The odd thing is that that is the way I always feel when one of my patients dies, but that's never the way it happens. Instead, at the funeral I greet the family, we hug each other and shed a few tears together, they forgive me, and I am given an honored place in the funeral ceremonies. It doesn't make sense. I was engaged to prevent death and now I've lost, yet I'm still honored. I'm always afraid that someone will catch on and some family is going to revolt, point a finger at me and cry out for all to hear, "He's a fake!"

I go to Betty's funeral. The family greets me with tears, hugs, and kisses. I sit in a pew and listen as her friends eulogize her, and I hear the priest promising her an eternal life of peace in paradise. As I leave, the family again thanks me for coming. For the first time in my life, I realize that I have lived with an illusion. Patients don't expect me to perform miracles. They leave that up to the priest. All they ask of me is that I do my best and offer them sympathy when I fail. If I had realized this before, I would have gone to many more funerals.

DECEMBER

I am back in full swing, my schedule is full, old patients have returned, and new patients wait without complaint in the wings. Again I have more consultations than I can handle. Lawyers seek my advice on defending malpractice claims. I am scheduled to give talks to professional groups all over the Northwest, and for this winter I have my choice of tempting medical meetings in Hawaii, Palm Springs, and Florida. There is an invitation on my desk from a pharmaceutical firm offering me a free trip to Bermuda; a few years ago, accepting a fountain pen from a drug house was considered unethical, but not today. I have all the trappings of success; I am back at the pinnacle of power. I should be happy, but I am not. Something is lacking.

In the past, the changes in medical practice have been gradual and evolutionary; during the past few years, the changes have been revolutionary. We used to be described as a cottage industry with each doctor doing his own thing, but now, suddenly, we are big business.

I am unhappy with the discussion at our hospital staff meeting this morning. We discussed marketing, public relations, and how to increase demand for our emergency room services so that department can become profitable.

I am unhappy that now I am being told by nurses and clerks whether my patient is sick enough to be admitted to the hospital and how long he or she can stay. All this is to meet the demands of Medicare, Medicaid, and other insurance companies, and it goes on in spite of the many reports of increased complications due to shortened hospital stays. Up until recently, only I could make a decision as to whom to admit and how long they would stay.

I am unhappy with the increasing practice of hospitals "dumping." If a patient appears at the emergency room and has no insurance or funds, he is sent on to the next hospital. I never believed that I would live to see the day when a hospital would turn away a patient. Hospitals have traditionally been nonprofit and have belonged to religious institutions or government. Now they are owned by corporations and are openly out to make a profit.

I am unhappy that the hospitals advertise. I heard an ad on the radio today: "Come use our Alzheimer's disease clinic." There is no treatment for Alzheimer's disease. The clinic is expensive, yet it can do no more for the patient than a good general practitioner and a social worker. At one time, this was described as quackery; now it is legitimate medicine.

I am unhappy with physicians' advertising. One medical journal, referring to the listings in the yellow pages of the telephone directory, labels it "yellow professionalism" and points out that many of the specialists are self-anointed and self-appointed. The journal suggests that although these ads probably benefit the physician, it is questionable that they benefit the patient.

I am unhappy with the restrictions placed by insurance companies and Medicare on what tests and procedures can be ordered for the patient. New terms have been introduced: cost-curtailment, cost-accounting, cost-effectiveness. Translated, these terms mean, spend as little money as you can on the patient; costs can become more important than saving a life.

Every generation feels that it faces a new problem, but medical costs were a problem when I was a student during the depression. Then we were taught to do intensive histories and long physical examinations in order to avoid the expense of laboratory tests and X rays. I have never forgotten the look on a widow's face when a professor said to her, ''Your husband died of cancer of the colon. We would have made the diagnosis earlier if we had done a colon X ray, but after all, that would have cost five dollars.'' People didn't sue for malpractice in those days.

I am unhappy with the malpractice crisis. Each year, more and more physicians are being sued. I have gone through years of practice without a malpractice suit, but statistically, that cannot go on much longer. With the present attitude, it is just about impossible to practice medicine without encountering a malpractice suit. It is not only the loss of money that is threatening, it is the damage to the psyche the physician fears.

I am unhappy with the unrealistic promises that we make and cannot keep. In spite of what we say, we can do little to prevent cancer, heart trouble, and strokes. The best we can do is try, but in many cases failure is inevitable.

When I started medicine, it was a profession dedicated to aiding mankind. The doctor was an autocrat, but his master was the patient. The patient hired him and the patient paid him, and in turn the doctor's efforts were dedicated only to the welfare of the patient. Today there are new masters: Medicare, Medicaid, the insurance carrier, and the business manager of the clinic.

Now doctors are becoming tradesmen, hired by big business and beholden to big business, not the patient.

I know now why I am unhappy. It is no longer fun to practice medicine. I suppose that if I had thought about it, I would have figured all this out a few years ago, when the practice of medicine began to change radically. Certainly the facts were available before I got sick. But coming back to my office now after being a patient for so long has widened my gaze. It has made me see my beloved profession differently.

LATE DECEMBER

T his is the time of year for celebrations, but I don't enjoy cocktail parties. I don't care for alcohol, and the noise drowns out the conversation, inane though it often is. Unfortunately, though, this is one party we are obligated to attend.

Dee and I are standing off to one side, wishing we were somewhere else, when a woman comes up to me, grabs me, hugs me, and kisses me full on the lips. Whatever my usual reaction might have been, this time I don't particularly appreciate the affection. After the radiation therapy, my vocal chords are denuded of protective membranes, and I am especially susceptible to infection. Besides, I don't even recognize the lady.

And then it comes to me. I didn't recognize her because I was looking at her through the haze of her gray hair and her wrinkled skin. But when she begins to talk, the haze lifts, and I see her as a young woman with shining blond hair, fair, with an extraordinarily pretty face. I return her hug enthusiastically, remembering Alice Thomas and her husband, Roger. We were all shocked when Roger died unexpectedly in his sleep some years ago, at the age of only forty-two. Not only was Alice bereft, she was also stranded by her husband's death—penniless, jobless, without any marketable skills. The first morning after he died, I spent a few hours on the telephone badgering people until I finally persuaded somebody—I don't remember who—to take a chance and give Alice a job.

Looking at her now, well-dressed and obviously prosperous, I can see that it has all worked out for her, and it delights me. That is one aspect of traditional medicine that some of us could be proud of—that before the days of medical office management you could take the time to do something financially "unproductive"—like thinking about the patient's life, not just his case.

JANUARY

Just after the New Year's holiday, I am sitting at Rose's Restaurant, eating a plate of smoked Northwest salmon, which seemed like the least lethal thing on the menu for a man of my age and circumstances. I am talking to a colleague, a doctor who is obviously one of the brilliant minds of his generation, about the technical and medical problems of a difficult case we've both been dealing with. One thing leads to another, and then I do the unforgivable: I begin to talk about feelings, to share with him some of my unease about the course of my own treatment.

"For God's sake, Ed," he says. "What are you complaining about? You're alive, aren't you? You had cancer, and you didn't die! Be thankful."

Of course he is right about that. In fact, it is what I would have said myself to anyone "whining" the way he must have thought I was doing. After all, if my grandfather had had my illness, he would not have survived it. If my father had had cancer of the larynx, he might have survived, but he would have had radical surgery and been left voiceless. As for me, I have had no pain and no surgery. I can talk and I am well, at least for now. I am, at the very least, in remission. My profession has probably given me more time—and, for me, that is no small gift.

But there is so much room for improvement, so many things that could have been done better for me—and that I could have done better for my patients. It is hard not to feel discouraged.

Except that things may be changing. Now that I am back at the doctor's lounge at the hospital, I listen to my friends and relatives, all colleagues, and I sometimes have to laugh. For what is happening with a lot of patients is making a lot of doctors mad.

Not me, though. I've switched sides. I welcome the new breed who isn't satisfied to take "three pills a day" but wants to know what they are and what side effects to expect. I'm glad that some patients are asking, when they make their appointments, "How long will I have to wait? When can I come in and be taken on time?" I wish there were more patients who would say to me, as one woman did several weeks ago, "I've just read an article in a health magazine that says there's another way to treat my illness."

I knew what she was talking about, and I had ruled out the treatment she referred to because the evidence that it worked was shaky and no one yet knew much about the side effects. I explained this to her but I didn't get angry at the question. I didn't answer her as if we were of a different species: I, *the doctor*; you, the patient.

Maybe that means I'm making some progress. Maybe this old dog can learn a few new tricks—in the little time that's left.

EPILOGUE

Early in 1986, I realized there was something else I'd learned during the year of my illness. The new lesson was: Edward E. Rosenbaum, M.D., is not indispensable. That is a revelation. During the time I was ill, the office, the clinic, the medical school, and the hospital all seemed to function without me—though not quite as brilliantly, of course.

The truth was, my practice now seemed too confining to me. I wanted to go back on the stump, not as I used to, under the auspices of the AMA, but writing and speaking as a doctor who is the patient's advocate, as a health care provider who has learned what it's like to be on the receiving side of the medical profession.

One night, long after Dee had fallen asleep, I slipped out of bed and groped behind the night table, fiddling around until I found the wire I was looking for.

Dee sleepily turned toward where I was crouched on the floor and said, "It's midnight. What in the world are you doing down there?"

"I'm disconnecting the phone. No more night calls."

To my horror, Dee began to cry. "How can you do that?" she asked. "People may need you."

"And I'm going to keep helping them," I laughed, finding her hand in the dark. "I'm going to keep helping them. It's just that I'm not on the night shift anymore."

ABOUT THE AUTHOR

DR. EDWARD E. ROSENBAUM was born and educated in Omaha, Nebraska, where he attended Creighton University and the University of Nebraska Medical School. His postgraduate training was at the Jewish Hospital of St. Louis, the Michael Reese Hospital in Chicago, and the Mayo Clinic in Rochester, Minnesota. He served in the United States Army in World War II as assistant chief of medicine of a mobile surgical hospital and during combat as a shock officer. He was chief of medicine of the Women's Army Corps. Dr. Rosenbaum entered private practice in 1948 and became clinical professor of medicine at the University of Oregon. He founded and was Chief of the Rheumatology Clinic at the University of Oregon Health Sciences University. He has four sons, three of whom are physicians, and six grandchildren. He lives in Portland with his wife, Davida Rosenbaum.